The Prosecutor and the

The Prosecutor and the Judge

· · · · · · · · · · · · · · · · · · · ·

BENJAMIN FERENCZ AND
ANTONIO CASSESE

INTERVIEWS AND
WRITINGS

¶

Heikelina Verrijn Stuart
Marlise Simons

PALLAS PUBLICATIONS

Cover design and layout: Maedium, Utrecht

ISBN   978 90 8555 023 5
e-ISBN   978 90 4851 133 4
NUR   828

© Heikelina Verrijn Stuart & Marlise Simons /
   Amsterdam University Press, Amsterdam 2009

Contents

Preface

Meeting Benjamin Ferencz
and Antonio Cassese

ANYONE WHO HAS met Benjamin Ferencz and Antonio Cassese knows that here are two men totally committed to the defense of human rights and human dignity. They are, by the strength of their personalities guides and tutors. They offer inspiration and an irresistible remedy against cynicism. Both men have many stories to tell about the power politics and self-interest of states and their leaders and about the excessive violence and cruelty individuals can commit when they have the opportunity. But they also teach us that one need not be a blind optimist to go in search of direction and progress through law. For them to believe this is of itself no small achievement, since their work has confronted them with human behavior at its worst.

This book is published to celebrate the Praemium Erasmianum awarded in November 2009 to Benjamin Ferencz, the former Nuremberg prosecutor, and Antonio Cassese, the first president of the International Tribunal for the former Yugoslavia (ICTY) and current president of the Special Tribunal for Lebanon. The prosecutor and the judge together embody the history of international criminal law from Nuremberg to The Hague. The choice to interview the laureates was based first and foremost on the wish to introduce these two remarkable personalities, well-known among their colleagues in the lively international legal community, to a wider audience.

The idea for this book is rooted in a book Antonio Cassese published in 1993. At the end of the 1970s, Cassese interviewed in depth the great Dutch international lawyer, B.V.A. Röling, who had been a judge at the Tokyo tribunal, the post Second World War International Military Tribunal for the Far East. For several reasons, the book was published much later, in the watershed year of 1993. In that year, the Tribunal for the former Yugoslavia was established by the UN Security Council to try the war crimes being committed in the heart of Europe. To this day *The Tokyo Trial and Beyond* remains a treasure trove of observations and wisdom: many of the issues Cassese and Röling covered in their conversations have lost none of their urgency. Cassese's connection with Röling was forged in scholarship and a clear-headed critical approach of international criminal law. By no coincidence, Ben Ferencz and Bert Röling also met in the course of their advocacy to have "aggression" properly defined by the United Nations. Both fiercely independent, they were deeply aware that every war brings about unspeakable horrors and grief and should be prevented by all available means.

The very first time I saw Ben Ferencz in action was in Rome in 1998. Within the span of five weeks the treaty for the International Criminal Court had to be hammered out. There was a strong sense of momentum, of now-or-never. Debates raged day and night, in the great conference rooms, in the back chambers and in the corridors. In the middle of it all Ferencz could be found, tirelessly canvassing unwilling or uninformed delegations. I saw government representatives, NGO members and journalists bestow their respect on this former Nuremberg prosecutor. And, Ferencz, who is not the most patient of men, showed an immense patience in his explanations of the complicated legal and political subjects at stake. The ICC founding treaty came to pass. The crime of aggression made it to the final text only at the very last stage of the negotiations. But the crucial issue of the court's jurisdiction over this crime was postponed. It may have been a blow for its champion, but Ben Ferencz saw it as another step forward, and he continued to explain, to lobby and to travel the world. It was hard to catch him in one place. With the review conference of the ICC looming in 2010, he moved from meeting to lecture to conference, from New York to Saint Petersburg to Salzburg, always on the same mission, delivering his mantra: stop war. And, most immediately, he urges his audience: make it possible for the ICC to prosecute crimes of aggression.

At times during the interviews, when we expressed our concerns about legal and human shortcomings in the burgeoning ICC, Ferencz plainly told us that we had our noses too close to the ground. We should take our distance. What may seem stagnation at the time can be seen as part of an important development with hindsight.

Antonio Cassese came from international humanitarian law and human rights law to the new field of international criminal law. At one point in the interview he told us: "The body of international law is made up of a set of rules that gradually emerge, and as a result the common conscience of mankind is found in customary international law." Cassese pairs his conviction that the law of humanity is anything but a stagnant, unmovable system with his own deep awareness that the dignity of humanity is not safe in the hands of the state. At the same time he has an open mind for the many efforts by individuals representing the state to do what is right. He has a keen eye for the beauty and the power of the language of criminal law, with its precise definitions and qualifications.

In his fourth report as president of the ICTY to the General Assembly of the UN in 1997, Antonio Cassese quoted from Benjamin Ferencz's statement given on 29 September 1947 in the Einsatzgruppen trial in Nuremberg: 'If these men be immune, then law has lost its meaning, and man must live in fear.' The judge sided with the prosecutor.

After some years in Florence, Cassese was once again drawn to the epi-centre of international criminal law, the Dutch city of The Hague, this time as president of the Lebanon tribunal. His life often shifts among his many roles from being a judge on the bench to leading the UN Commission of Enquiry on Darfur and then again to periods with a different perspective as scholar, teacher, editor, commentator and writer of innumerable articles and books. But never do these changes bring about disconnection. Cassese keeps his nose to the ground, to use the words of Ben Ferencz, and com-bines a talent for seeing and thinking through the themes of international law with great clarity and command of detail.

On the wall of his office we found a text by Bertolt Brecht: "Von Natur bin ich ein schwer beherrschbarer Mensch. Autorität, die nicht durch meinen Respekt entsteht, verwerfe ich mit Ärger, und Gesetze kann ich nur als vor-läufige und fortwährend zu ändernde Vorschläge, das menschliche Zusam-menleben regulierend, betrachten."(I am by nature a man who is difficult to control. I reject with outrage any authority that does not rest on my respect. And I regard laws only as provisional and soon to be changed proposals for regulating human intercourse). It speaks for itself and for Cassese.

About the book

MARLISE SIMONS AND I share a long history of working closely as report-ers at the international tribunals and the ICC, Marlise as a correspondent for *The New York Times* and I as a contributor to law journals and Dutch radio and television. Now, in this project we found a great way to pool our resources.

Of course, when we suggested the interviews, both Cassese and Ferencz protested that they had written extensively about every imaginable subject relating to international law, to the laws of warfare, humanitarian law, hu-man rights law and international criminal law. We only had to pick and choose from their work. And in general, there is an abundance of publications about the international tribunals, the International Criminal Court and any subject related to the stormy development of this area of law. But, quoting from Cassese's Preface to *The Tokyo Trial and Beyond* we retorted, what better medium is there than 'the oldest and noblest means of communication: word of mouth'?

And so we met with Ferencz in Florida and with Cassese in The Hague. Over the course of several days, we sat for long hours of questioning, discussing and contemplating, but also laughing, gossiping and being utterly chaotic. The interviews were far too long and freewheeling, in the same way as Cassese described the result of his interviews with Röling. And after much pruning and reordering, trying to make sense, we ventured to send the draft text to our interviewees. They reacted in character. Ferencz preferred to discuss changes by telephone and said he was too occupied preparing new seminars. Cassese not only added to the text and clarified any vagueness, but also meticulously corrected errors and typos. And both were more than willing to answer additional questions. So ultimately this has become their book, and we can only hope that they will consider it a worthy present on the occasion of their Erasmus Prize.

To further paint the portraits of the prosecutor and the judge, we have chosen articles written by the laureates themselves, some older, some from a more recent date. We could have just published the extensive bibliographies and referred to the website of Benjamin Ferencz where every article and lecture and the more personal "Benny stories" can be found. However, we wanted to underscore the interviews with some of their own texts offering a link from the past through the present to the future. The selection of articles could be considered random, but we have looked for texts that are related to subjects covered in the interviews.

Since the legal definition of aggression in war and, ultimately, bringing the crime of aggression under the jurisdiction of the ICC have been a life-long obsession of Ferencz, the obvious choice was one of his articles about this theme: *Removing the Lock from the Courthouse Door. Reconciling Legitimate Concerns*, published in May 2008.

Ferencz's heartfelt wish that an effective compensation system for victims of war crimes in the broadest sense would one day become possible is backed by the choice for his article *Compensating Victims of the Crimes of War*, dated 1972. And lastly, we have chosen some chapters from his so-called Benny stories about a complicated and troubled period of Ben Ferencz's working life. In *Seeking Redress for Hitler's Victims (1948-1956)* he offers us a glimpse, not yet the whole story, of an under-reported post-war period. Ferencz is one of the very few who was there, who can tell us about the aftermath of the Second World War from his own experience, not only about the Nuremberg tribunal and the *Einsatzgruppen* trial, but also about the restitution system that he practically invented in Germany to compensate victims and their relatives for some of their losses. Here the man who stood in the middle of it all, grappling for a rational solution in irrational circumstances, gives us an insight into the many questions he had to face then and which are all too recognizable in our time. Today, the ICC is struggling to find a balance between functioning as a criminal court and answering the dire needs of the countless victims of the massive violence. The ICC Trust Fund for Victims in particular will be confronted with many of the complications Ferencz touches upon in this series of stories.

Antonio Cassese published his *Soliloquy* earlier in *The Humanitarian Dimension of International Law, Selected Papers*. It is his personal history as a scholar and as a practitioner of law, and it is a great pleasure that we were allowed to add this beautiful article to the book. Cassese covers the latest developments in international justice in his recently held lecture *Reflections on the Current Prospects of International Criminal Justice*. From the abundance of articles about court decisions and the merits of international criminal law, we have chosen, and we admit that we could have just as well have picked one of the many others, the article called *Is the bell tolling for universality? A plea for a sensible notion of universal jurisdiction*, published in 2003. It covers the intricate matter of universal jurisdiction, the sovereignty of states and immunities of the senior state officials, which we explored further in the interview with Antonio Cassese.

Heikelina Verrijn Stuart

The Prosecutor: Interview with Benjamin Ferencz

Heikelina Verrijn Stuart and Marlise Simons

Einsatzgruppen Trial; the Search for Evidence

Question: You were the prosecutor of one of the most compelling Nazi trials in Nuremberg, dealing with the execution of more than a million people. Yet the trial took place almost by chance. How did you become the prosecutor?

Ferencz: After the war, I returned to Germany again as a war crimes investigator. I had done that work during the war, as the concentration camps were being liberated. But in 1946 I was sent to Berlin to set up a branch of investigators. Our staff went to scour for evidence in the ruins and in the buildings that were still standing. The Foreign Ministry, the Treasury, the ss offices, the Army, the Navy, all of these offices were in Berlin. We hired a staff of about 50 people, including some former German refugees. We had people combing through the American zone. In their respective zones, the occupying powers of course had complete access to whatever remained of such things as archives. We found ruins; we found pieces. It was quite remarkable when you found something quite intact. The Nazis had tried hard to destroy their records, but they were so methodical in their record-keeping that much was left.

Q: What type of important documents were discovered?

F: One tremendous find was a little villa in the woods of Dahlem, near Berlin. From the air, it looked like a little cottage. Underneath were subterranean chambers blocks long, holding some 10 million Nazi party files. They included application forms of everybody who applied for admission to the Nazi party, every officer in the ss, their letters of promotion, their letters of recommendation, all intact. Staff at special centers in London and in Paris sorted and analyzed such files for evidence to be used in Nuremberg. They pulled documents that might be relevant for the trial of the Nazi leaders, which was already going on at the International Military Tribunal (IMT) in Nuremberg, and also for the trials that we were still planning.

Q: What trials were these?

F: After the trial of the Nazi leaders, the four occupying powers could not agree on additional joint trials, so they authorized further separate trials in their respective zones. The United States wanted proceedings to present the bigger picture of the war. The thinking was that we could not judge the events of a civilized country like Germany without bringing in all the other component parts of society, the lawyers who perverted the law, the generals who planned the campaigns of aggression, the ss who committed the atrocities, the doctors who performed medical experiments, the industrialists and financiers who seized foreign properties and used slave labor. These became the so-called 'subsequent trials'. Telford Taylor, a Harvard lawyer who had joined the IMT prosecution team, was put in charge. They were held in the same courthouse in Nuremberg.

Q: You were not assigned to any specific trial?

F: No. And the *Einsatzgruppen* trial, where I became the prosecutor, had not been planned for. It would not have taken place, except for the extraordinary luck of discovering the records.

Q: Can you describe this?

F: In the spring of 1946, Fred Burin, a Swiss national and one of our diligent researchers, came to see me. He was very excited about papers he had found in an annex of the Foreign Ministry, near the Tempelhof Airport. He showed me three very big, heavy, loose-leaf folders. It was a set of reports sent by the Gestapo office. Judging by the distribution list, they were distributed to the high echelons of the Nazi and military hierarchy. The reports had an innocuous title like 'Operational Situation Reports from the Soviet Union'. But every page was marked: Top Secret. And here, done with typical German efficiency, were the daily reports of the executions done by the *Einsatzgruppen*. These were the special ss task forces that followed the German army as it moved east, attacking the Soviet Union. Officially, their assignment was to establish 'security', but they were plain murder squads.

Their real mission was to kill the Jews, the Gypsies, Communists and many other people defined as dangerous. Now we had found their records, almost complete, just one or two days missing. Amazing. The reports started in June 1941 and covered every day for about a two-year period. There were detailed accounts from the four groups, divided into A, B, C and D, and their various commandos. They listed what towns and villages they entered as the German army advanced into Poland, Ukraine and further into the Soviet Union. What they had done in those towns. How many Jews and others they had eliminated, transported, liquidated, cleansed the town of – or other such euphemisms, all of which meant murdered. They rounded up the people, let them believe that they were being taken to a work camp or resettled, and then took them to a hidden place and killed them, usually by firing squad. Most victims were shot, and later on they gassed people in vans. We had some indications of this during the IMT trial. But we didn't see the total picture until we put the whole thing together, and that was possible as a result of one of the researchers finding the records. So we had the names of each town and village, the date, the number of people killed, the name of the unit, the officer in charge, and other officers. I sat down in my office with a little adding machine, and I began to count the people that were murdered in cold blood. When I reached a million, I said that's enough for me. I flew from Berlin to Nuremberg, to see Telford Taylor, who by then was a general. And I said, we've got to put on another trial.

Q: You took those records with you to Nuremberg?

F: I took samples. And the rest I closed and put them in a sack, like a US Mail sack. And I turned them over to Colonel Helm, the commander in charge of the documentation center. I told him, you safeguard these, nobody gets into these, they're vital evidence. When I saw Taylor, I said here is a clear case of mass murder of a million people, and we know the names of the units, the commanders. And he replied, that's tremendous, but we can't put on any more trials. All the lawyers are assigned. The program for prosecutions is fixed. We don't have the budget for it, we haven't planned it, it has to be approved by the Pentagon, we don't have staff. I became exasperated, and I said, 'We cannot let this slip, these people must be tried'. I offered to handle it. Taylor asked if I could do it in addition to my other activities. I said sure. So, I thereby became the chief prosecutor in what was later called the biggest murder trial in human history.

Preparing for Trial

Q: This was your first trial. You were 27. What did you do next?

F: My wife and I moved from Berlin to Nuremberg, a badly destroyed city. I canvassed other trials and managed to put together a team of four lawyers. Then we sent out requests to the Allied war prisoner camps, listing the names of officers who were the most prominent in the documents. We asked that they be sent to the Nuremberg prison. There were 3,000 men in the *Einsatzgruppen*. We had many of them. But we could only try a symbolic number. We chose 24 because no Nuremberg trial could have more than 24 defendants. The reason was there was room for 24 people in the dock. So we started with 24 defendants. In the end we tried 22 because one died, and one committed suicide.

Q: Because the *Einsatzgruppen* were most active on the Eastern Front, in the Soviet Union, in the Baltics, Belarus, Ukraine, did you ever consider handing over all this evidence to Soviet prosecutors?

F: Not a chance, no chance whatsoever.

Q: Why not?

F: Because the Cold War was already on. Relations between the Soviet Union and the United States were not good. The Soviet method of dealing with such prisoners was to disappear them; we don't know what happened to them. The best example that stays with me personally is when we were advancing toward the East, the Russians were coming West, and we met out somewhere near Weimar. Oh, it was a joyous occasion, the American troops met the Russians, we were drinking vodka and dancing. One of the Russians asked me: what do you do? I said, I'm a war crimes investigator. He asked, what does that mean? I said I had just come from Buchenwald, I had investigated, would make a report and hold the people for trial. And the Russian said, don't you know what they did? I said, of course. And he said, then why are you asking them questions, why don't you just kill them? And I said, no, we don't do that. We'll give them a fair trial.

Q: Churchill and Roosevelt at first also wanted summary executions of the prominent Nazis. For a while, only the French and the Soviets wanted to put them on trial. Anyhow, you saw no chance of a fair trial if you were to hand over the *Einsatzgruppen* evidence to the Soviet side?

F: None whatsoever. As a matter of fact, there would have been instant trials, which I also witnessed in the concentration camp. Inmates got hold of guards and beat them up and killed them, or burned them alive. Many were killed. The scenes were indescribable.

Q: You also did not have a high opinion of the Dachau trials done by the US Army?

F: I was originally interviewed for the Dachau trials. They were quite separate from the proceedings at Nuremberg. The Dachau camp was used as the site, and the trials were by American military commissions. Among the defendants were camp commanders and guards from places we had liberated, Buchenwald, Flossenberg, Mauthausen. I was there for the liberation, as a sergeant in the Third Army, General Patton's army, and my task was to collect camp records and witness testimony, which became the basis for prosecutions. Trials also involved German civilians who had killed American prisoners or downed Allied pilots. But the Dachau trials were utterly contemptible. There was nothing resembling the rule of law. More like court-martials. For example, they might bring in 20 or 30 people, line them up, each one with a number on a card tied around his neck. The court would consist of three officers. None of them had any legal education as far as I could make out; it was coincidental if they did. One officer was assigned as defense counsel, another as prosecutor, the senior one presiding. The prosecutor would get up and say something like this: We accuse all of you of being accomplices to crimes against humanity and war crimes and mistreatment of prisoners of war and other brutalities in the camp, between 1942 and 1943, what do you have to say for yourself? Each defendant would be given about a minute to state his case, which was usually, not guilty. One trial for instance, which lasted two minutes, convicted ten people and sentenced them all to death. It was not my idea of a judicial process. I mean, I was a young, idealistic Harvard law graduate.

Q: Nobody protested against this?

F: Nobody protested, including me.

Starting the Trial
....

Q: The trial where you were the lead prosecutor, the *Einsatzgruppen* trial, began in September 1947. Were there experts to whom you could turn for advice?

F: We had no people around. We were just our small team. There was no time. We did not need much advice. We had all the documents, all the evidence.

Q: Early on, Robert Jackson, as the chief American prosecutor, had spoken of the need to establish 'incredible events' by credible evidence and to use a maximum of documentary evidence to avoid the suggestion of Allied propaganda. He deliberately limited the use of eyewitness testimony. What did you do?

F: The prosecution rested its case after two days. We had all the proof, all their own reports.

Q: And you called witnesses?

F: I didn't call any witnesses, for a very good reason. I may not have had any experience, but I was a damn good criminal law student at the Harvard Law School. And I know that some of the worst testimony you can get is eyewitness testimony.

Q: The worst?

F: The worst! We had camps full of displaced persons all over Germany. I could have called any 50 people and said, here are my 22 defendants, do you recognize any of them, did you see any of them commit crimes? All fifty of them would tell me, yes. And they would believe it. I didn't need that. I had the reports, and I could prove the validity of the reports, although they challenged them, of course.

Q: Today prosecutors working in war crimes tribunals sometimes speak with envy of the great paper trail available in Nuremberg, the immense records of the Nazi bureaucracy. They may face the opposite situation, having to build their cases around many witnesses, insiders, and circumstantial evidence.

Even in the trials of former presidents, like Slobodan Milosevic and now Charles Taylor.

F: They may get no confessional documents because they have to rely on the governments. Governments may be silent because they were complicit.

Q: You were leading your first trial ever. Did you need approval from Telford Taylor, who was then in charge of all the so-called subsequent trials?

F: Taylor was an outstanding jurist, really high caliber. But a cold fish, very aloof: A hard man to get close to, but a thoroughly decent man. He had given me the job, he had sent me to Berlin. He just told me to clear the indictment with Jim McHeaney, a young lawyer, good lawyer, who was in charge of trying the cases against the ss. We had no separate Pentagon clearance, so we stuck the *Einsatzgruppen* into the ss cases. One afternoon I sat down with McHeaney for two hours or so. That was it. I sent Taylor an advance copy of my opening statement. He usually made the opening statements, but not this one. He let me make it, a young kid. He only changed one word. I had written, 'Vengeance is not our goal, nor do we seek retribution.' He put in: 'a just' retribution.

Q: On the opening day you said that every man in the dock had committed horrendous crimes with full knowledge and intent. And you used a phrase that has been repeated over the years: 'If these men be immune, then law has lost its meaning, and man must live in fear.' So you took two days, but the defense went on for months. What went through your mind then?

F: Many things. Every defendant was provided with two lawyers, paid for by the court, and they were given copies of everything. The defense produced affidavits by the bushel. Everyone had excuses, saying they were forced, they were following orders. They said that the reports were falsified. Or that the numbers of the people killed had been inflated to please superiors and so on. There were times when I felt outraged. For example, the day one defendant, a colonel, said: 'What, Jews were shot? I hear that in this courtroom for the first time.' We had the records of every day that man was out murdering, and he had the gall to say that. I was ready to jump over the bar and poke my fingers into his eyes. There were other issues. Every time I raised an objection, the chief judge, Michael Musmanno, overruled me. Every time. And I was getting very annoyed and thinking he was a fool. At one point he even said, don't keep raising all these objections. The defense can introduce any evidence it wants, anything up to and including the habits of penguins. That became known as the penguin rule.

The Sentencing

Q: Did you think this lacked balance?

F: Well, the day of the sentencing, I realized that all along he knew they were lying. I arrived early in court; I was the first one there. It was a very grim, very quiet moment. The courtroom filled up, the three judges arrived in their black robes, facing the wall that had a panel that could open up. The defendants were brought in this way from the prison below the courthouse. The panel door slid open. 'Prisoner Ohlendorf'. s s General Otto Ohlendorf stepped forward, put on the headphones. Then he heard: 'For the crimes of which you have been convicted, this tribunal sentences you to death by hanging. Next one.'

The judge handed down worse sentences than I would have imposed. So he had made up his mind, early on, that he wasn't going to be deceived. For him the question was how to sentence them. He was a devout Catholic, and he went into a monastery for a week before sentencing. He convicted all 22 people, and of these he sentenced 13 to death by hanging. During the trial, he had let everyone say whatever they wanted to say. He gave so much leeway; he was leaning over backwards to show the world that it was a fair trial. In the end, his was a very fine judgment, 175 pages, spelling out the basis for each judgment, but also full of human understanding and compassion as well as advancing the rule of law. He did in that judgment everything I would have wanted him to say and do.

Q: In hindsight, was it important that he gave the extra time?

F: Yes, he was right.

Q: You hadn't asked for any sentences. Why not?

F: You may ask, why didn't I ask for the death sentence? I'm not against the death penalty. I felt very deeply about this, I could never figure out a sentence that would fit the crime. It was so grotesque, a crime of such magnitude. You could not balance the lives of these 22 people in the dock against the million they had killed. There was no way to find any balance or justice. Taylor, who made the closing statement, asked for no sentence either. He asked for firmness rather than leniency for the terrible crime against humanity.

Q: Just recently you saw a documentary film about the *Einsatzgruppen* called *The Masters of Death*, and you said it even included footage of the death squads at work in the Ukraine. It is amazing that these scenes were filmed, presumably by people close to the killers. And you saw this 68 years later.

F: This was the first time that I saw this happen in reality. For the trial, I had all the reports, all the documents. But I did not know any footage existed. There were scenes from Babi Yar. The people shooting were probably members of the *Einsatzgruppen*, and the victims varied. Many families, children looking frightened, but no screaming. They were lined up and gunned down. By rifle fire, one bullet at a time.

I did not show any film at the trial, I had seen none, and I had none. But I would have put this on during the trial. I would have used it. To think that if we hadn't had the luck of finding the documents, there might not have been a trial at all.

Q: During the trials, Germans did not pay any attention to the Nuremberg proceedings, according to journalistic accounts at the time. Your trial ended in April 1948. Did it get much press coverage outside Germany?

F: In retrospect, it's quite remarkable how little attention that trial got at the time. While the trial of the Nazi leaders was going on, it overshadowed everything else. And when it was over, public interest also disappeared. The press was already bored. During the subsequent trials, there were a few correspondents attending the opening statements and the judgments. But in between, the seats for the audience were usually empty. Germans were not interested in watching. They didn't feel vindicated by the trials. They were seen as victors' justice. Germans had their daily concerns to provide themselves with bread and board.

Q: Did you regret that lack of interest?

F: The most disappointing of all my war crimes experience was the absence, the total absence, of any expression of remorse on the part of any defendant. Maybe Albert Speer is a separate case. But that is a different discussion.

Remorse; Visit to the Prison

Q: Would it have made a difference if any of your accused had shown re-morse?

F: I think I wouldn't have tried him. I was prosecuting people who tried to justify their crimes. We had many prisoners, we could have put hundreds of people from the *Einsatzgruppen* on trial. We had identified many. The no-tion that the Nuremberg trials were doing justice is inaccurate. It was only a small sampling.

The judges probably would have been more lenient in their sentencing if they had seen remorse. One important consideration was always, what ex-cuses did the accused have? I think it is one reason why not everybody was sentenced to death.

One of our accused wrote a letter saying: I see now the horrible blasphe-my, which was committed. And he committed suicide in his cell.

Q: After the sentences were handed down, you have said you went to the prison to see your most important defendant, General Otto Ohlendorf. What made you want to do that?

F: I had never wanted to talk to any of the defendants personally, not to be influenced by any emotional response to the person. I thought I will judge them on the basis of my documents. My researcher would go to talk to him, and I'd give him my questions.

Ohlendorf was an ss general, the commander of *Einsatzgruppen* D. At trial, he had been relatively honest, and he admitted he had killed 90,000 Jews, although he claimed his men sometimes bragged about the body count. He was an intelligent, well-educated man, who had made some good legal arguments, trying to show he had no criminal intent. He did his duty as he saw it, without questioning Hitler who had said that Germany was about to be attacked by the Russians. That was the excuse they all used.

After he was given the death sentence, it was my idea to go and see him. I wanted to do this, I was sort of saying goodbye. I looked for some remorse, some recognition that he had done wrong. I knew he had a wife and five children, and I felt sorry for them. So I asked him in German if there was anything I could do for him, some small favor.

His response was that the Jews in America would suffer for what I had done, and that he was right. He was almost spitting in my face. He had no remorse. On the contrary. So I just said: 'Goodbye Mr. Ohlendorf,' and I left.

I never saw him again, but I saw pictures of him dropping on the noose and lying in his coffin. Landsberg prison had wanted me to be there and do a show. But I wouldn't go, so they sent me the film.

Victors' Justice; Clemency

Q: Do you think the trials at Nuremberg were victors' justice?

F: No, they were not. If we wanted victors' justice, we would have gone out and murdered about half a million Germans.

The top people, Robert Jackson, Telford Taylor, and many of us at the Nuremberg court were not trying to get revenge, but to show how horrible it was, in order to deter others from doing the same. And to be just, not to convict anybody unless there was absolutely clear proof of their guilt. This was the main principle. It wasn't perfect.

But Nuremberg firmly and properly defined aggression as an international crime. It helped to develop crimes against peace and crimes against humanity.

Q: Criticism of the Nuremberg trials has included the fact that some crimes were defined for the occasion, after the fact, that some had not been charged before.

F: That criticism is unfounded. The law is not static and is adapted to meet the changing needs of society. That was recognized by the courts. The Nuremberg judgements considered those arguments, and they were systematically and validly rejected. There was nothing unfair in charging the defendants who must have known that their evil deeds were criminal. It would have been unfair to let them escape.

The IMT judges ruled: 'To assert that it is unjust to punish those who in defiance of treaties and assurances have attacked neighboring states without warning is obviously untrue, for in such circumstances the attacker must know that he is doing wrong, and so far from it being unjust to punish him, it would be unjust if his wrong were allowed to go unpunished.'

Q: Did that criticism apply to your trial?

F: The judgment included 55 pages analyzing the validity of the law. But it can be put briefly. The prosecution had not invented the crime of murder, or mass murder. And the judges wrote: 'Certainly no one can claim that there is any taint of ex post factoism in the law of murder.'

Q: After the trials, the Americans ordered a sweeping act of clemency, some say to placate German public opinion as Cold War tensions rose. Many of the people tried by the US had their sentences commuted and were released early, so that they served a decade, or less. From your trial, only four of the 13 death sentences were carried out.

Telford Taylor was angry and called it a blow to the principles of international law and the concept of humanity for which the war was fought. What was your reaction?

F: The sentences of all of the so-called subsequent trials had to be reviewed, that was part of the rules. But the review commission did not in any way challenge the facts found in the trials. John McCloy, the US High Commissioner for Germany, had given secret instructions that the trial facts were to be respected. We did not know about those instructions at the time. Taylor and I were partners then at a law firm, and we argued about it. He said the motives were political. I told him I knew McCloy. It was McCloy who had to sign the death warrants. He used to be a business lawyer, and he told me once he had never sentenced anybody to death in his life. To sign a paper saying, hang them, I knew he had difficulty with that.

Some sentences were changed for humanitarian reasons, some to balance the discrepancies in the sentencing.

Nobody asked my opinion. But my view was if punishment was imposed for good reason, it should not be reduced without good reason. In most cases there was no good reason that I was aware of. Afterwards I told McCloy what I thought of his Christmas present to three important *Einsatzgruppen* boys. And I pointed out that he had freed Nosske, the man whom the other defendants called the biggest bloodhound of them all.

Allied Bombing of Cities
....

Q: After the war, you worked in Germany, among the ruins of Nuremberg and Berlin, and you saw many other cities bombed by the Allies. Both the Nazis and the Allies used large-scale attacks on civilians, yet bombing was not included as a war crime. Did you ever think that the Allies, while fighting a just war, also deserved criticism or punishment for bombing so many civilian targets?

F: No, no, I never had such feelings.

Q: In the very same week, in August 1945, when the Allied governments signed the charter for the Nuremberg court, Washington dropped two nuclear bombs on Japan and destroyed the cities of Hiroshima and Nagasaki. Was this irony ever discussed in Nuremberg?

F: Yes. In response to complaints that Americans bombed Leipzig and Dresden and the other cities, and dropped the nuclear bombs on Japan, Telford Taylor's response was: responsibility for the atrocities of total war rests not on those who end the war, but on those who start it.

Q: That argument provides a carte blanche to do anything in between. How can that be acceptable?

F: Sometimes you are in the unfortunate position of having to make such a choice. There's no good solution. It's the least worst. If it meant that Japan would never go to war again, and have that same effect on others, then it would be justified.

Q: But driving through the ruins of all those cities that were not military targets...

F: I'll give more examples. In the last days of the war, I was sent to Würzburg to find Karl Haberstock, Hitler's art dealer who had confiscated so many paintings in Europe for Hitler's museum in Linz. It was just after an Allied air raid, and the city was still smoldering. Most of it was destroyed. From a distance, it looks like it's standing, you see the walls, heavy brownstone walls. And the walls are standing, but there's nothing in between. Phosphorous bombs hit the roofs, they burn with great heat, they burn out the ceilings, they drop down to the next floors, they burn, they drop down to the next floor, until they hit the basement. Everything inside the building is dead and burned. And I look at the city; smoke is still coming out of the buildings. Very, very grim. I can still see that picture. And I found Haberstock in the prison. Most of the prison was destroyed, but the basement was intact. I took him out and set up an interrogation centre in the house of a family whose son was buried in the backyard. Very grim feeling.

And in France, in Normandy, we got off the beach and moved toward Saint Lo. The heavy bombers of the Air Corps come from England to take the town. Like rain in a storm, the sky is black with bombs. Saint Lo becomes a pile of rubble, by which I mean you can't identify any house in Saint Lo. There are still a few steeples standing, somehow chimneys seem to survive the bombing. You can't find a road, you can't find a house, you're riding with tanks over the rubble. It was a city! The city is gone. And this was in France, our Allies.

My reaction to seeing this type of destruction? I didn't blame ourselves for it. You know what I blamed ourselves for? I have visited every American military cemetery I could – even Russian cemeteries. And I always pause at the cemetery gate thinking, is this really necessary? And, who's to blame for this? I was never convinced that any of this was necessary, never. And I visited the old World War I cemeteries in Verdun, and the battlegrounds of the Marne. And the conclusion is always the same. We must stop war. We must stop glorifying war. We must face the horrors.

Albert Speer

....

Q: You mentioned earlier the case of Albert Speer, the Nazi minister of armaments and war production.

F: An interesting man, a close associate of Hitler. His deputy was executed, but he did not get the death sentence. The judges at the IMT never said this, but my sense is that the judges saw in Speer a sense of remorse. After he had spent 20 years in prison in Berlin, I wanted to talk to him. I was writing a book, later called *Less than Slaves*. In the book I described my efforts to get compensation from German industrialists for the slave laborers they had been working to death in their factories. And all of them had denied that they had any slave labor, they denied that conditions were bad, they denied the persecutions, they argued that it was all necessary, that there was no choice, that the workers were well-treated, there were no atrocities, the food was good, etc.

Speer was the architect of the programme. He had signed the orders. So I asked Speer how he explained those denials. Speer answered, 'They were lying.' I said, 'Can I quote you?' 'Yes', he said. So I told him, 'I will send you the draft of my book, if there's anything wrong with it, please correct it. I want to state nothing but the complete truth.' Speer agreed, and I sent him the draft. He marked every page '*einverstanden*', agreed, agreed; he changed nothing.

When I first arranged to meet him secretly, at Frankfurt airport, I thought, I'm taking a risk. He's liable to tell me, get lost, I've served my twenty years, Mr. Prosecutor, your days are over. The fact that he didn't do that, and his willingness to answer, confirmed to me that he wasn't just being deceitful at the trial. He was showing some sense of remorse. Many Germans don't agree, they say he was clever, he outsmarted the Americans. But because of this experience that I had with him, after the war, I believe that on this point he was sincere.

Justice and History

Q: Going back to Nuremberg, some scholars believe that one purpose of the trials, and other modern post-war trials, is to establish the record and thus construct the collective memory. Do you believe that?

F: No, that should not be the purpose of trials. Collective memory is important, and trials can help. They present the evidence. But in a context of courtroom confrontation and hostility, it is better to leave history to the historians. They come later, create the museums, read all the documents, have a more objective frame of mind to consider them carefully.

Q: Of course prosecutors select from events what they need to prove their case, so inevitably that does not produce the full record. All the same, numerous trials were held about events in Nazi Germany, Japan, Yugoslavia and Rwanda. Louise Arbour, speaking about her experiences as the chief prosecutor of the UN tribunal for the former Yugoslavia said: 'The courts cannot provide the historical record, because history leaves room for doubt, it can be revised. But justice binds itself to a permanent and official interpretation of facts, because it has a need for finality.' Do you think that these two methods of enquiry clash?

F: I quite agree with the sentiments. We don't know what is justice, and we don't know what is history. So not only do they not clash, they run parallel in their uncertainty. There is no such thing as absolute justice; there is no history, which cannot be written in another way.

Q: And going back to the trials...

F: The question comes back, where was the justice in the trials after the war? You have selected people who you happened to catch, against whom you happen to have documentation. You cannot really speak of justice. You can only point to the horrors of this type of criminal behavior and where it leads. You can hope that by showing the suffering, there will be some deterrent effect.

Inspiration

F: My career goal was crime prevention. My parents were poor immigrants from Transylvania, and I was raised in Hell's Kitchen in New York, a high-density crime area with many juvenile delinquents. As a young boy I wanted to become a law man, to help prevent crime. That was my aim. Not to punish criminals. By the time a crime has occurred, you've already lost your case. You have to deter the crime, before it occurs, all the more so in connection with war.

Q: When you were young, who were some of the people that influenced your thinking?

F: As a young boy I had been much impressed by Mahatma Gandhi. I spent time studying all religions – I was taken by Buddhism. When I was about fourteen, fifteen, I'd go to listen to the sermons of the Ethical Culture Society in New York, run by a German refugee, Felix Adler. It was an ethical, sort of religious movement. They impressed me; they did not talk about what somebody said 3,000 years ago. I had a lot of great teachers. At City College of New York, Morris Rafael Cohen was a teacher of philosophy and a great mathematician. He taught ethics, except what impressed me was that he was rather cynical in his outlook.

Q: Did you appreciate that?

F: I admired that in Oliver Wendell Holmes, one of the judges I have most admired. He would say: to get at the truth, we must bathe everything in cynical acid. Another man who was important to me was Morris R. Cohen. He insisted: don't accept the slogans and the symbols, which will only confuse the mind. A flag, whatever flag it is, is only a piece of cloth on which they've painted various symbols. Yet, if someone burns that cloth, they can kill you for it. Cohen would take slogans and symbols which were taken for granted, take them apart, analyze them.

The most impressive judge I studied at Harvard Law school was Benjamin Nathan Cardozo, a man I never met, but he certainly influenced my life. He impressed me very much with his analytical skills, and the beauty of his decisions, they were almost poetic.

But I had two renowned professors at Harvard. One was Roscoe Pound, an amazing man, the most renowned international jurist then. I tried to work for him. When that didn't work, I offered my services to Professor Sheldon Glueck, who taught criminology. I got the job. Since Glueck was preparing a book on German aggression and atrocities, my first assignment was to research legal precedents in every book in the Harvard library that related to war crimes. That probably changed the course of my life.

There was another remarkable man, Professor Zachariah Chafee. He espoused human rights long before human rights was offered as a subject, and he taught ethics.

The law we were taught then was very different. We learned that to pay fees only upon the success of a case was both immoral and illegal. When I see what lawyers are doing today, I'm so shocked. I'm shocked when lawyers are looking for clients, and you hear on the radio: 'You have a complaint, you don't feel well? Come see us, we specialize in complaints against hospitals, against doctors' and so on. When I went to law school, that was considered a crime that could get you disbarred. It's the crime of champerty, which lawyers today have never even heard of: It's the crime of soliciting clients for your own enrichment, encouraging clients to sue. Unfortunately, those teachings have become eroded or forgotten with the passage of time; the legal profession and the public are the worse for it.

A Soldier in the War

....

Q: Were you drafted while at Harvard?

F: I had a scholarship, and I was about to be drafted. But someone, without my knowing, may have changed my life. The dean had given me a letter for the draft board, asking for a short deferment. So I thought I had to go into the army six weeks later. But I could complete my studies. After graduating, I went back to the draft board because I was very nervous about it. The same clerk was still there, and I said I'd been waiting to be called, but I wasn't. He followed me out into the hall and asked how I made out in law school. I said I made out all right. He asked if I needed another extension to pass my bar exam. I didn't understand.

Then he told me he had been a soldier in World War I, a captain in the Air Corps. He limped; he said he had lost a leg. He told me he was drafted while at law school and had never been able to finish his studies. He had regretted it all his life. So he said that when I arrived, he thought he would not let the same thing happen to me. I did not know this, but he had put my file in a drawer and held my records until I finished law school. He allowed me to become a lawyer, and a war crimes investigator. I never saw him again.

As an enlisted man I was sent to join the invasion of France in General Patton's army. When we had finally fought our way to Germany, I was put to work to collect evidence of the horrors of the concentration camps. Unbearable horrors.

Compensating Victims

....

Q: The time you spent in Germany forever changed your life, you have said.

F: Many events during the war, and after the war in Nuremberg, have influenced my life. But I think the greatest contribution I made was in the field of restitution and seeking compensation for victims. The Military Government had issued a law for the restitution of heirless property. It was based on the principle that you should not be able to murder people and keep their assets, too.

When the trials were over, I was approached by a consortium of the world's leading Jewish organizations, including the World Jewish Congress, British and American groups, B'nai B'rith and others to handle restitutions.

But there was nothing in place, no mechanism, no organization. Restitution was untrodden ground. There was no precedent. I had to start from scratch.

The board of directors of the Jewish consortium all wanted to show they were doing something. They did nothing, except hold a few meetings. It was troubling that some were more concerned with their own prestige than with the gravity of the issues. And they would not put up any money because they did not quite believe the efforts would work. There was just enough to pay my salary. So I borrowed money from General Clay, Commander-in-Chief of all US forces in Europe. I asked him for a loan from the American share of the Occupation funds. Later, I also borrowed money from McCloy, who succeeded him as US High Commissioner. In the end, McCloy even cancelled the debt for the Jewish victims. These two men played important roles and really bent the rules to help.

I made myself director-general of the Jewish Restitution Successor Organization to impress the Germans with a title. We got started by requisitioning army jeeps and offices. With the funds we borrowed, we hired people and issued instructions to go through every real estate registry in Germany. Any transfer of property after 1933, claim it. If there's a Jewish name there, claim it. If there's any doubt, claim it. Clay gave me a four-month deadline. On the last day of that filing period we filled up an Army ambulance with 163,000 claims. That was just the start.

It was the start of what became a ten-year struggle, involving secret negotiations, treaties, lawsuits and appeals. We won the principle that heirless and unclaimed property taken from Nazi victims could be retrieved by a charitable organization that would benefit survivors in a wider sense.

To help the claimants, we set up a group that became the world's biggest legal aid society, the United Restitution Organization, with offices in 19 countries. Over one million claims came in, because it covered not only Jews. The laws we negotiated were for the benefit of everybody. It was not based only on Jewish claimants, there were of course Catholic victims, gypsies were victims, victims of all kinds. We also negotiated the Reparations Treaty between Israel and Germany.

The restitution question was immensely complicated to administer. We developed principles for compensation. The procedures and decisions made a lot of people very angry. We were accused of all sorts of things. There were charges that we were stealing funds. My biggest shame is that I paid my staff so poorly.

I was the director of three organizations, they divided my salary into three parts, and I could not live on it, I had to go home. The consortium had been prepared to invest $5000 in salaries. When I left, they had 50 billion marks for the victims. By then, in 1956, there was a huge organization, I had a staff of 1200 people, with 250 German lawyers and offices in every major German city and 19 countries. I remained as a legal advisor and kept going back and forth. Germany later set up another fund, the Foundation for Remembrance, endowed with $5 billion. And some payments are still going on as part of German disability pensions for past injuries. In 2001, a victims' organization reported that the restitution programs had benefitted 500,000 survivors in 67 countries, Jews and non-Jews.

It was a tough problem, retribution. It's not well known, because we did not spend a penny on public relations. I have written little about it. It's highly technical, involves a multitude of legal issues. In the book *Less than Slaves*, I touched on it, but not in detail.

What I learnt is that individual claim programs did not work. Too drawn out, too many imponderables, too much anger. We aimed for bulk settlements instead. And we could only aim for material claims. That was our struggle. How do you make good? How do you measure? There was no answer, but I learnt some bitter lessons.

Painful Lessons

Q: What do you mean to say?

F: Those who suffered the least got the most. They had other avenues. Those who suffered the most received the least. The victims of the Communist countries, there were many, got nothing because they were in the wrong place. We had no dealings with Eastern Europe. The excuse was that West Germany did not have diplomatic relations with the East.

And another issue: whatever the program, the money must go to the victims, not to the lawyers. The lawyers in the final settlements from Germany, around the year 2000, got three, four million dollars each. But no claimant got more than $10,000, maximum. I found that thoroughly disgusting.

Q: Who were these lawyers?

F: Jewish lawyers from New York. They listed their hours. The lawyer who bragged loudest that he was acting pro bono ultimately demanded four million instead of three million. From money that came from funds destined for the victims!

Q: It was meant for survivors of the camps?

F: For survivors of anything. It was shocking. I was holding my nose. But I deliberately turned my back on Holocaust problems after I did the *Less than Slaves* book. I'm now preoccupied with trying to prevent the next Holocaust.

Compensating Victims and the ICC

Q: Compensation for the victims is now part of the mandate of the ICC, and it has become the subject of intense debate.

F: They do not understand what the size of the problem is, how complicated it is. You cannot compensate for great suffering. It can't be done. You cannot measure pain, you cannot measure fear, you cannot measure the damage from rape, and you cannot price human life.

Q: But where should they start?

F: They have to start with the principle. They have to start with the judgment of Judge Pal in the Tokyo trial, because he concludes it's all our responsibility – we let it happen. You must begin with philosophy: who is responsible for what. Then if you want to go into law, law operates on a principle of cause and effect. The one who causes the harm is responsible to compensate the victim who suffered the harm. That's the basic principle of legal compensation for injury. Now what do you do when the person who caused the injury has no money, it happens all the time. Then you say, the Valdez case – the captain was sleeping in his cabin, he let the first mate drive the ship into the ground, he spilled the oil, the company should pay two million dollars. That's called the deep pockets theory of justice. Who has the money, pays. The Pal theory is: the whole world pays. After the massacre in My Lai during the war in Vietnam, just one man was convicted, Lt. William Calley. An action for a compensation of 400 million dollars was brought against

Calley, the Secretary of Defense and the Secretary of the Army by a group in Vietnam and was dismissed by the US District Court in Georgia. The legal reaction to the crimes committed by the US military was less than adequate. States are not eager to prosecute their own soldiers, and compensation is seen as an acknowledgement that war crimes were committed, so that is dismissed.

Q: At the ICC there is a second pillar, the Trust Fund for Victims (TFV), that is meant to support, compensate and help victims in various ways, not necessarily with financial support. The TFV so far is concentrating on areas where ICC investigations are going on. But the intention is also to support victims of crimes with no connection to the accused or crimes before the ICC.

F: If support from the Fund is decided in separate proceedings, then it is already partly disconnected from the court itself: It will be a struggle to find funding. The central question remains: who compensates victims of the crimes of war? There is only one answer for me, and that is stopping war. And help people in need, regardless of the cause of their suffering. What difference does it make for a man's hand if it was hacked off or lost in a hurricane? So you don't give compensation linked to a fault of some individual, but for the failure of all individuals, for our failure to build a system and an organization, to minimize terrible human loss and tragedy which happens over and over again.

Q: And the ICC permits victims to participate in a trial, even at its earliest stage.

F: As long as not all victim groups join, but act through a responsible representative, then that's a good idea. Victims should be heard. One of the biggest complaints against me when I was in Germany working on the restitution for victims of the Nazis was that victims were not involved. The problem was, no one was available who could speak dispassionately as a victim. People were hardly alive; they were blinded by their hatreds and their own needs and fears that would make them a disruptive factor in difficult negotiations with an unwilling partner. And so I represented them, as did my staff. But the victims did not really understand that.

Q: Rehabilitation is another aspect altogether.

F: It's enormously complicated. Take a person in a war-ravaged region who was not injured or raped, but is starving to death or has no medical care. The ICC Trust Fund does not want to treat victims of war crimes or of post war poverty differently, they want to assist a village or a group as a whole, but that requires a very skilful operation in an utterly complex situation.

Q: Should the compensation mechanism be completely outside the court?

F: You need a legal decision to determine who is responsible for the injury, and the nature of the injury. Who must pay, how much and for what? This is a highly technical, drawn-out process, which must be outside the normal court mechanism. Whatever it is, it must be a simplified procedure. And relatively speedy. If not, the victims are dead by the time you get around to it. And the money must not go to lawyers, but to the victims.

Campaigning for Peace

Q: After your return to the US, you spent many years campaigning against war, and you are still campaigning and writing and lecturing.

F: I hate war. I hate war in my bones. I've seen war, and I know what it is about, and we must eliminate it. It is the greatest evil of all. Eisenhower knew it. All the generals know it. We must stop glorifying war. Break out of this mania. Stop the hurrahs with the flags and the music. I know I stand alone on the hilltop, screaming. People say I'm crazy. I'm not crazy. The crazy people are the people who make war.

In an interconnected world, with its rapidly accelerating technology, we cling to the same ideas of sovereignty. We have to change the mindset. That is what I have been working on. We have to stop war.

Q: Now you are almost 90.

F: I cannot stop. It's a trauma, I'm sure it's the trauma of what I saw. We have not built the institutions we need for a peaceful world. It seems we haven't suffered enough. In the First World War, 20 million people were killed, and we got the Covenant of the League of Nations. It was very weak. After World War II, and 50 million people were killed, they gave us the United Nations Charter. Very weak. Then perhaps after millions more, people will wake up and say: we have to build more institutions. One of the institutions we got is a court, the ICC. But it's too weak because nations don't give it the support it needs.

The Crime of Aggression

Q: And one of your campaigns is to make the crime of aggression a punishable crime in the statute of the new International Criminal Court.

F: It's outrageous that for the crime of aggression, 'the supreme international crime', there is no international court that has the competence to deal with it. We must fight to make sure the crime of aggression will become part of the jurisdiction of the ICC. I'm an individual, with no government or organization behind me. But I keep talking and writing to make sure that nations do not repudiate the Nuremberg conclusion, namely that war-making is the supreme international crime because it encompasses all the other crimes.

Q: How do you see dealing with the crime of aggression? How will it work if it comes under the jurisdiction of the ICC?

F: The prosecution for the commission of the crime is easy. You say, Look you have used armed force against x and y and z. You have no authorization to do that from the Security Council of the United Nations. Period. Now a practical matter is, what is it really going to mean? For the time being, not much. How many aggressors will we stop? Not many. Hitler would not have been stopped by that, and I think many others wouldn't. But some of them will be. And it will begin to catch on. And once in a while, we'll bring them in, and we'll try them.

Q: Can the prosecutor investigate and prosecute *ex proprio motu*? Or will he need a trigger from the Security Council?

F: He certainly does not need a request from the Security Council. On the contrary. The big argument is about that, because the Security Council wants to control the show. The Security Council has already given away the game. They cannot change the Charter of the United Nations which holds that it is for the Security Council to determine whether an act of aggression by a state has occurred. It's not up to the Security Council to determine the guilt or innocence of an individual, but it can determine the context, which is commission of an act of aggression by a state.

Nobody can say that there is no clear definition of aggression in law. The British Law Lord Bingham of Cornhill hit the nail on the head when he stated in a 2006 case, '... the core elements of the crime of aggression have been understood, at least since 1945, with sufficient clarity to permit the lawful trial (and, on conviction, punishment) of those accused of this most serious crime. It is unhistorical to suppose that the elements of the crime were clear in 1945 but have since become in any way obscure' [see: Jones, R. v. (2006) UKHL 16 (29 March 2006)].

But despite assurances built into the UN Charter and the Rome Statute, some powerful states still hesitate to accept the jurisdiction of any new legal institutions to deter aggression. They are holding on to outdated notions of national sovereignty. As long as the military may be called on to intervene with armed force in situations, which political leaders claim are purely defensive or humanitarian, then commanding officers can hardly be expected to welcome the existence of any international court to test the legality of their military action. Their concerns are fully understandable.

It may be that the Security Council will not respond to a request from the Prosecutor for guidance about whether an act of aggression has occurred. But even then, an indictment will serve a useful purpose.

Aggressors should realize that there is a possibility of trial before the ICC. The deterrent effect, no matter how modest, is an improvement over the present state of immunity. Surely, something is better than nothing. Even if the aggression issue lies dormant on the Council shelf, the Prosecutor need not remain helpless. National leaders suspected of planning or committing the crime of aggression may simultaneously be charged with crimes against humanity and war crimes - which carry the same maximum sentence as aggression. There has never been a war without atrocities. At the ICC, prosecuting crimes other than aggression requires no prior permission from the Security Council. The Council's failure to react to aggression is bound to evoke public outrage. The court of public opinion, informed by new means of instantaneous worldwide communication, is a powerful force that cannot long be ignored or suppressed. The 'shame factor' may be the most effective enforcement tool available to the ICC.

The UN Charter prohibits the use of armed force without Security Council approval. Violent disputes that seem irreconcilable are best resolved by a court of law competent to administer justice and hold lawbreakers to account. To be sure, there have been many occasions where the Council was politically paralyzed, and force was needed to save human lives. The rules for humanitarian intervention, as NATO said it did in Kosovo, and the criteria for legitimacy are still in the formative stages.

Q: You have criticized the use of force that is justified by fine rhetoric, but in the end remains unlawful.

F: Yes, inventing new legal terminology to evade criminality, such as calling it 'soft law' or 'illegal but legitimate' or a 'responsibility to protect', can be a dangerous practice. Still, the states should not be so afraid of the ICC. Not every instance of use of force will be prosecuted. There is ample room in the existing ICC Statute to cope with illegal acts that might be morally justifiable. The ICC Statute recognizes that there may be many valid moral reasons, including intent and knowledge, for limiting criminal responsibility or mitigating punishment. The Prosecutor, subject to the control of judges, can decide not to prosecute if it 'would not serve the interests of justice'. Judges can acquit, and the Security Council has no say in the matter. Penalties and sentencing 'must reflect the culpability of the convicted person'. Court sentences must 'take into account such factors as the individual circumstances of the convicted person'. The ICC recognizes that morality and the law go hand in hand.

Too much has been already given away. The Security Council is authorized, under Article 16 of the ICC Statute, to stop the court, to suspend the investigation or prosecution for a year, and every 12 months they can renew it; they can repeat it for 20 years. They've given the independence of the Court away to the Security Council. So, if the Security Council wants to stop a prosecution of the crime of aggression, it can. But more is already given away in the Rome Statute. Article 121, section 5, is a very important but obscure potential barrier against the prosecution of aggression, if it were to be defined in the Statute. Any clear reading of it leads to just one conclusion: that if an amendment is passed regarding the crime of aggression, the state is only bound if it ratifies the amendment. So in fact, they have given the right to prosecute crimes of aggression away already in Rome in 1998.

Q: And 'they' are...?

F: They are any of the member states, or any state in the world, that does not want to be bound by the ICC amendment until it has ratified the amendment. They are the big powers, who want to decide for themselves whether they attack or not, whether they wage war or not. I say: 'Leave it to the judges'. And I say to the big powers: 'What are you afraid of? Stop stomping on the small countries. You've got them tied up hand and foot, and you still insist upon rubbing their nose into it. You want to have a free hand to commit aggression? Go ahead, commit your aggression. See where it gets you.'

Q: So, in theory, it would be simplest if first the Security Council determines that State X has committed aggression. Then the prosecutor can choose any individuals he deems accountable.

F: And if the Security Council has not acted, the prosecutor's hands are tied for the moment. Then the prosecutor can investigate and determine for himself whether there was aggression or not from one state to another and that the Security Council has failed to act. And the prosecutor and we can all say: shame. Meanwhile, we will sue them for crimes against humanity and war crimes and hold them in jail forever on those counts. But isn't it a shame that the Security Council has failed to do its job for 50 years.

Room for Immunity; Protective Intervention

Q: Do you see any room for immunity in international law? The ICTY and the Special Court for Sierra Leone have both ruled that no immunity agreement or amnesty can be admitted before their courts where charges of war crimes, crimes against humanity or genocide are involved. Do you see any situation where immunity could be acceptable?

F: Not for immunity. There is room for something else, and this has been ignored and perhaps we need to spell it out, and that is using force as part of the responsibility to protect. There are situations in international law where you know what is the right thing to do, and you cannot, because you don't have the arms to do it, or you're not getting Security Council support because of political reasons, and yet you feel something must be done. The classic example is Sarajevo and Kosovo. People, civilians, are being shelled; they are being killed by aggressors. The Security Council refuses to act, or is unable to. If you use force without its authorization, it's illegal, a violation of the charter. I discussed it with David Scheffer, who was then the US Ambassador for War Crimes issues. His response was: we cannot let the people die.

I said, you have to let them die. Because if the rule of law dies, many more will lose. I have regretted that opinion. I have changed my mind on that.

I believe there are situations where there is a responsibility to protect. They came up with a nice title for it: 'humanitarian intervention'. But it was too difficult to codify, to differentiate between humanitarian intervention and aggression disguised as humanitarian intervention.

Q: And that's what you wrote about: illegal force with 'good intentions'.

F: Yes, in the context of the ICC, which is what you are asking about, there may be a situation involving the responsibility to protect. It would require that the amount of force is restricted to the amount necessary to achieve that goal, that you have exhausted every other remedy without success, that you will cease as soon as possible and get out, and that it is clear you are not seeking an advantage for yourself or your country. Under those circumstances you could do what you have to, in order to protect people, knowing that you are violating the law.

Q: And this would provide immunity for a leader?

F: I am against immunity. But what happens then? Possibility number one: The prosecutor is authorized under the statute to take all circumstances into account. The decision to proceed or not is up to him. He can say it is not criminal behavior, but behavior to save human lives. Possibility number two: The judges reach the same conclusion. The prosecutor may say he is obliged to prosecute, to put the facts on the table. The judges then examine them and say: although it is a violation of the law, we will exercise judicial restraint. We issue a suspended sentence for violating the law under these circumstances.

Q: So the question is settled in the sentencing.

F: That is correct. If the judges do not take the motivation into account, the prosecutor can file an appeal. So you have an opportunity there for intelligent, decent judges. The judge is not there to punish people for noble behavior, but for evil behavior. In the sentencing they can acknowledge that the law is deficient in not being able to distinguish that type of case, except in the punishment procedure. So there you give effect to what they called: it was illegal but lawful.

It is an old ecclesiastical principle. Don't use more force than necessary to achieve the objective and cease as soon as you can. And it's the measure of last resort.

Q: At the International Criminal Tribunal for the former Yugoslavia and the International Criminal Tribunal for Rwanda, all sides, all parties to a conflict can be prosecuted. At the ICTY, most cases have involved Serbs, and the ICTR in fact has only prosecuted one side because the current government, and its foreign supporters, are opposed. Could the same happen with the crime of aggression if the ICC had jurisdiction, that is, prosecute all parties to the conflict?

F: Absolutely. The law applies equally to everyone. It's a fundamental principle. It is not only about the first shot. Aggression can be faced with other aggression. Failure to stop when the enemy has been defeated is also aggression. That's the question of proportionality.

Q: Countries that are afraid of the power of the ICC can use the argument of complementarity. They can deflect any action by the ICC by prosecuting the crimes at issue at home. They have the right of first refusal.

F: If I were at the Department of Justice in Washington, I would introduce a little bill saying any crime that was listed in the Statute of the ICC is subject to punishment by federal courts of the United States. Period.

Q: But states are not willing to prosecute their own leaders.

F: No, except if there's a change in government. But then, in many countries, they'll kill the old leaders. Often you'll have to wait. Transition takes time.

Q: First it was only possible to hold states responsible. Then international criminal law became a booming business, and the attention shifted to individual liability. Shouldn't states also be confronted again?

F: State responsibility cannot be ignored, but it's met by reparations. Individual responsibility is met by individual punishment, and whether reparation will be useful or not depends upon the circumstances. We learned in World War 1 that if you demand too many reparations, you're going to create a World War II. But there is a clear distinction. You cannot punish a state. Crimes are committed by individuals, not by states. States can be held accountable financially, by reparations of various kinds, as was the case in Germany.

Q: But prosecuting a sitting or former head of state, like Omar Al-Bashir of Sudan and Slobodan Milosevic of Serbia, is also a way of striking at the state. Inevitably, it means more or less indicting the state.

F: I don't know how you go after a sitting president if you want to respect the principle of sovereignty. You can only promote a revolution against a president by his own people, which is the way it is often being done. The CIA's pretty good at that.

Q: There is an arrest warrant out there now against the sitting president of Sudan.

F: What makes you think that you're going to have the court move forward without problems? To begin with, there is no international military force. True, as long as Al-Bashir is there and has not been locked up, he will be defended and protected by the state. It is not possible to go in and declare war on Sudan in order to get him out.

Q: The argument is made that the state can be stigmatized and excluded from the political peer group.

F: I don't see stigmatization as a very productive approach, and anyway it creates more hatred.

The Rome Treaty

Q: How did you feel on those last days of the Rome Conference in 1998, when the ICC finally became a fact?

F: I was elated, I was elated.

Q: Even when they negotiated away the crime of aggression?

F: Oh, I was delighted that it was in. It was very close. The representative of New Zealand grabbed me, and she said, you have to go down and talk to, I think she said, Syria. She said, they're going to kill aggression. I said I don't know anybody from Syria. She said, you have to go and talk to them; they're going to kill aggression. So I ran down to the meeting room, and this guy grabs me and says, 'Closed session, out!' They threw me out.

If they had not included aggression, I'm sure the whole thing would have failed, collapsed. So it was hanging by a thread, and the trick compromise was that sleight of hand. That's what they did; they said aggression is in but it's out. Hocus pocus. It's in, but the court can't act on it unless you stand on your head and do all kinds of impossible things.

But still, it was in! That was the step forward; it was a small step forward. Because to not have it in would have been a repudiation of Nuremberg, as if the Nuremberg principles were victor's justice and applied only to Germany, and Tokyo's principles only to Japan. That would have been a terrible blow. I had had so many arguments before that time, with competent lawyers saying forget it, you're going to sink the ship, you'll never get it, and you're going to drag everything down with it. And I said, I don't care. I'm going to fight for it.

People say I'm crazy with my campaigns to make aggression a crime, to work for a more peaceful world. They say it will never happen. There have been some fantastic steps forward in the evolution of humane thought. We had slavery, and then we ended it. We never had women's rights until they became a fact. We never had international criminal courts before; we never had a black American president before. We never had the Internet before. Change will happen. It takes patience.

Can International Criminal Law Deliver Justice?

Q: You have talked about the arbitrary nature of events in Nuremberg, the trials of people you happened to catch, the space available in court. The number of trials you scheduled. This obviously also confronts today's international tribunals, albeit on a different scale. Does that make international law less valid, or valuable?

F: It makes it less effective, but not less valuable. The value is there, the ability to enforce that value on a greater scale, and to carry it out and have it adopted as part of the customs and habits of a people. That is the goal that we hope to achieve by using these examples. Without that value, you're condoning the wrongful behavior.

You're pointing to the problems to which we have not yet found adequate solutions. But what you do is you do the best you can under the circumstances. I have given the example of the German de-Nazification proceedings, which are generally regarded as not very successful.

In the end, you certainly don't get perfect justice, it's imperfect no matter what you do, but it's better than no justice.

I always believe responsibility starts at the top, not at the bottom. It's not the private on the firing squad who pulls the gun who is responsible. It's the head of state who says we must eliminate all of our opponents, even if he never leaves his desk.

When a person has assumed a leadership position and is capable of directing mass crimes, it is not a given that he will be deterred by laws. There is a learning process, even at the highest level, and there is some deterrent effect. When the British were considering joining the United States in the war against Iraq, the head of the British military said, I'm not going unless I'm sure its legal. I don't want to end up in the dock like Milosevic. So we see the deterrent effect right there.

Iraq

Q: You were given an ovation in 2005 at the American Bar Association when you said that President George W. Bush and his leading cabinet members may have distorted the facts and committed the crime of aggression when invading Iraq: Do you believe there will ever be any legal consequence?

F: It's up to the lawyers. Everyone is entitled to a presumption of innocence. In my address I said that we have an obligation as lawyers to ascertain the truth. If as appeared from a London *Times* report, the president and members of his government may have lied to the country, knowing the facts they used were wrong, then it's our duty to investigate the facts. We're not under Goebbels here. The United States is a great democracy. In my judgment, the use of armed force without Security Council approval constitutes the crime of aggression. Other competent lawyers have another view. The public is entitled to know the truth. That's what democracy is about.

Criminal Tribunals Face Difficult Tasks

Q: Today's international courts face difficult tasks because, up to now, they have rarely had a paper trail, they are far from the scene of the crime and have to work in different languages. They have needed many witnesses who often come from great distances, and they may need special protection and anonymity.

F: All of the tribunals are in a difficult spot for very many reasons. Take the ICC, the statute is full of loopholes, full of requirements that are almost impossible to meet: to prove knowledge and intent, to prove the events themselves, to get the right witnesses, all that is very difficult. They have to cope with translations, foreign tongues. Many hurdles have been built into the statute: filters, pre-trial hearings, different chambers of judges, the right to appeal for hearings, to other pre-trial judges. Persons and nations that didn't want the court created all these hurdles deliberately to sabotage the court. They wanted to kill the court! So it's almost a miracle that we have a court. But it's quite an achievement.

You want perfection? The cathedral of the law can only be built one stone at a time. Patience and time. You do not build a cathedral overnight. You have to step back. I have a vision of fifty years. It makes a difference.

We must reread the decision of Judge Pal, 500 pages, in the Tokyo trial, in which he says: we are all responsible. We let it happen. We built a society in which we let it happen. We are responsible for Rwanda. That is a clear responsibility, we let it happen after the Holocaust. We knew it was going to happen, or a good chance that it would, and we did nothing. Our failure to condemn aggression, I put that in the same category. We are encouraging this. We have the means to stop aggression, and we don't. So where is our responsibility?

Q: We have many laws but without courts to enforce them. And there are courts without powers to enforce the law. Is that proof that international treaties and courts are no more than good intentions and political posturing? Laws cannot be enforced or apply only to the weak?

F: Right. A court or a law without enforcement is a farce. The truth is, countries don't want to give up the right to go to war when they think they should. It's about their power, and they don't want to give it up. And they have not been persuaded that it's in their national interest to do so. We have multiple treaties and agreements. All of them have loopholes, opt-out clauses.

Q: How do you see the continuing efforts of the Red Cross, of others working to uphold the Geneva Conventions and The Hague Convention, their striving for more humane behaviour in war?

F: Humane war? Humanitarian war? Of course it is very laudable that people try to minimize the horrors of war. But it is absurd to assume you can have a humane war. It does not exist. You go to war, you know what it is about. It's about killing the other guy. And if you have to kill his family and everyone around him, and all his neighbors, and his city, and his country, well so be it. War itself is the greatest crime, it is the greatest atrocity. It encompasses all the other crimes.

Q: Do you believe international laws and humanitarian conventions and the international criminal courts that apply them are all just a form of shadowboxing?

F: There are already enough nuclear weapons around to kill every living thing on earth. Now I believe that the military capacity exists in cyberspace to knock out all the electrical capacity on planet Earth. All Internet capacity, all thermonuclear capacity, all water purification capacity, all computers, all telephones. The capacity exists to destroy the entire electrical grid on the planet. That means, all the life-sustaining capacity. And people want to talk about humane war?

Q: So then, are all the rules of warfare outdated? Are they useless?

F: The rules we have do some good, within limits. They are ignored, bent, broken, whatever. But let us always remember that they will be cast aside in the heat of battle. They have served to mitigate situations to some extent. We don't use poison gas, at least not if we can be caught. We don't often go into a hospital and shoot the prisoners.

The law is an act of faith. But we have to believe in the deterrent effect of the law.

The Judge: Interview with Antonio Cassese

Heikelina Verrijn Stuart and Marlise Simons

Early Days at the Tribunal in The Hague

Question: Can we take you back to 1993, when you became a judge, and the first president of the International Criminal Tribunal for the former Yugoslavia? Louise Arbour became prosecutor a few years later. Referring to the two of you, she wrote about those early years: 'We had both been re-incarnated as characters in a very complicated play.' How complicated was it?

Cassese: We faced quite a few problems. The most obvious were that we had no budget, and little support from governments. Madeleine Albright has often said that in the Security Council, she was the only one out of 15 ambassadors who really believed in this tribunal. She said nobody thought that the tribunal would take off because it was seen as a sort of poor fall-back solution. That's why there was no budget. And that's why we could not pressure the UN.

The comparison with Nuremberg was obvious. There, Justice Robert Jackson only had to phone the American general in charge to ask for logistics, interpreters, secretaries, documents, evidence and so on. The tribunal was in an occupied country and had the whole US army behind it. So as the first international tribunal set up after Nuremberg, we immediately saw the huge gap between the enormous means available to the judges there and the total absence of means for us.

But I strongly opposed giving up. I argued that we could not kill what Claude Jorda from France and I often called '*une magnifique aventure morale et juridique*'. I said if we go home now, then we will never establish this precedent, and we will never know if we can apply international criminal justice. This helped us to wait for New York to decide.

I received great support from two people. Madeleine Albright supported us not only morally, but she also used her authority in the Security Council, and she had the US delegation put a lot of pressure on the General Assembly to adopt a budget.

Boutros Boutros-Ghali, the UN Secretary-General, was also extremely supportive. He came to The Hague in February 1994. At a dinner for him, I was to give a speech, so following tradition I provided my text in advance. My speech apparently convinced him that I was profoundly committed to this new idea of international justice. I was told that when he read it, he said: 'Then I have to change my own speech.' And his speechwriter prepared a new version, not the usual exchange of niceties.

Q: And you laid out in your speech...

C: The huge moral challenge we faced to lay the foundations and meet the needs of modern international justice. And the obligation we had was that we could not fail, because through us, the whole international community would fail. I strongly felt that our failure would also mark the end of any international criminal justice.

Q: And Madeleine Albright?

C: She came on her way from Bosnia to New York in January 1994. I was alone because all the judges had gone home to their countries. It was a Sunday, and she spent half a day with the whole delegation, including David Scheffer, her legal adviser who later became the American ambassador at large for war crimes. We had a lot of discussions, and as I was seeing her off, I asked her what she thought of trials in absentia. I had prepared a memo. I was very much in favor of trials in absentia, because we couldn't afford to have our tribunal paralyzed by fugitives or people in hiding. We had no police force. So we had to proceed with or without a defendant in the courtroom. I remember vividly that she stopped and said: 'Mr. Cassese, I'm not a lawyer, I'm a diplomat, but I can tell you that if you go for trials in absentia, you're making a mistake. Trials in absentia will be perceived in the US, in the UK and all common law countries as something wrong, morally wrong. In the US constitution we have a right to be present at trial, which is a deeply rooted right.' I dropped the idea. The next day the trials in absentia were dead.

However, I urged my fellow judges to accept some sort of legal provision for the eventuality that one or more senior indictee should remain at large. My colleague Sir Ninian Stephen, an outstanding Australian judge, thus proposed the substance of what then became Rule 61. While not strictly a trial in absentia and not providing for a finding of guilt, it allowed the court to receive and preserve prosecution evidence and have another look at the indictment (which had already been confirmed by one judge). Thus, the procedure was intended both to bring the charges preferred against the accused before the full Trial Chamber (consisting of three judges) and to publicly expose those charges. The Trial Chamber would then, by issuing an international arrest warrant, call upon all states to assist in bringing the accused before the tribunal. The President in his turn could alert the Security Council about any state's refusal to cooperate. It was very innovative. Prosecution witnesses and other evidence could be presented, as we did in the summer of 1996 in the case of Karadzic and Mladic.

A Prosecutor; Hard to Find

Q: So although you faced many obstacles, you had two of the most important allies you could have had, the American Ambassador and the Secretary-General of the UN. That's no small matter.

C: Right. Eventually, Boutros-Ghali simply asked me: 'Tell me what you need.' I said, 'Of course we need a budget, but especially we need a chief prosecutor.' The civil law judges - the Chinese, the French, the Egyptian and myself – thought it was appropriate to start work with the present deputy prosecutor because he could initiate proceedings and had the same powers as the prosecutor. But our common law colleagues felt differently. They argued that only the chief prosecutor himself can delegate his functions, and in his absence nobody can take any action.

I spent months, from January until late June 1994, phoning people in Latin America, in Africa, everywhere. One day I came across a French judge, Roger Errera, who had just been with South African friends in London who had fled there because they opposed apartheid. He mentioned Richard Goldstone, who had an impressive history and had headed the Goldstone Commission. I asked if Goldstone was Jewish? And he said: 'I refuse to answer that question as a matter of principle.' I explained I was asking because to us, a Jewish prosecutor would be excellent because we would have to deal with Catholics, the Croats, with Muslims, the Bosniacs, and with Orthodox Serbs. So a Jewish prosecutor would be an outsider. And I told him that, perhaps by coincidence, none of the four judges from Muslim countries were

Muslims. The Pakistani judge was Zoroastrian, the Nigerian was a Protestant, the Malaysian was a Hindu, and the Egyptian was Catholic.

Q: And what were you?

C: I was brought up a Catholic, but I'm an agnostic, and I respect any religion. My wife is Jewish, but she is also secular. And he said; ' I still refuse to answer your question.' So I said, never mind, I will phone him. Finally, I reached Goldstone, and he sounded interested.

Q: But Goldstone wasn't very eager to get the job.

C: Right. He said that Nelson Mandela had just appointed him to the constitutional court of South Africa. So Boutros-Ghali phoned Mandela. Mandela agreed to lend Goldstone to the tribunal for just two years.

And so a few days later, Boutros-Ghali had a proposal for the ICTY chief prosecutor. The Security Council adopted it unanimously. That Friday evening at 8:00, I got a phone call that Goldstone had been appointed. I was all alone in the tribunal, and I typed – very badly because I couldn't use the computer very well – a letter to all the judges who were away in their own countries, in Texas, in Australia and so on. 'Dear friends, *Habemus papam*.'
I faxed this letter to all of them. I was so excited that I barely slept that night. It was a great success. In one week, between Monday and Friday, we had managed to get a prosecutor. And why? Because Boutros-Ghali was so good. He understood.

Judges from Different Law Systems;
Writing the Rules of Procedure and Evidence

Q: Were all the problems solved by then?

C: No, on the contrary. Inside the tribunal we were eleven judges, some with an excellent judicial record and others who lacked a judicial background. There were national judges who had always been judges in their own countries, like Gabrielle Kirk McDonald, an excellent federal judge in the US, the Pakistani judge Rustam Sidwa who was on the Supreme Court, Judge Sir Ninian Stephen from Australia, whereas some judges, from Egypt,

China, myself, had never been on a bench. But we knew the international framework - we knew the treaties, the Geneva conventions, human rights law and so on. The Pakistani judge was extremely competent and a splendid man who had spent his whole life in Pakistan. So anytime we had a problem to discuss, he would pick up his Pakistani legal book, 'Dear colleagues, the solution is very clear, it is here in article so and so of the Pakistani criminal procedure.' And I would say: 'Judge Sidwa, my friend, you cannot think that we are in Pakistan. We are in The Hague at an international tribunal. So we can't apply Pakistani law. We have to take into account your law but also the American, French, Egyptian, Chinese laws, and so on.'

Unlike the ICC, we judges drafted our own rules of procedure and evidence. It took about three months, and it served as an important learning process for a new institution. It is something the judges in Nuremberg and the Tokyo tribunal also lacked, because the rules of procedure and evidence had been drafted by the four allied countries in Nuremberg and by MacArthur and his legal advisors in the case of Tokyo. The judges did not have this moment of collective education, collective training, and a collective exchange of experiences and adjustments. Each of us had to adjust to the experiences of the others. And then this process of collective learning and reciprocal intellectual adjustment proved to be crucial.

The only country that had already proposed a draft set of rules was the US.

Q: How much of the document the US presented was changed and how much survived?

C: The people from the civil law countries made quite a few changes. It largely reflected US procedure, without a jury, because we were professional judges. But in a trial where the prosecution has the examination in chief, the cross-examination and so on, the judges had no say. For instance, we suggested that the judges should be able to ask questions at any time or call witnesses, something that is not admissible in American law. We judges from civil law countries agreed that we should try to take the best elements of our own systems and to try to inject them. But the basics remained common law.

Cassese, a Prosecutor?

Q: In one of her comments, Louise Arbour said that you should have been the prosecutor, and she should have been the judge. Could you see yourself as a prosecutor?

C: No, but what she meant, and she was right, was that I was very pushy. I was always prodding the prosecutor. I was so impatient, in a way; I was even more pushy and inquisitive than any prosecutor. She probably felt that I lacked distance, coming from a civil law country where there is no water-tight division between prosecutor and judge. Perhaps I was over-stepping my duties as a judge. But I explained many times that I was not only a judge, passive and waiting for the prosecution. I was acting as a president of an international tribunal. Leadership meant to push for action also. I was the only one with a pass able to go to Goldstone's office. Other judges were not allowed to go up to the prosecution floor. But I would go up almost every day and talk to Goldstone when he was not travelling. Of course we never talked about specific cases – this would have been utterly improper. We spoke about his prosecutorial strategy, so that I could among other things decide quickly to what Trial Chamber to assign the forthcoming cases.

Q: You recalled the educational experience of judges sitting together and writing the rules, exchanging thoughts and experiences. It's completely differ-ent now at the ICC of course. Judges come in, and a readymade system awaits them. That is normal in every criminal court. It has its rules, judges come in, and they simply have to work with the system. But is there something lacking now? The spirit of pioneers?

C: When the statute for the ICC was drafted, of course the writers knew of our experience, and they knew that we had drafted and amended our rules about 30 times. But they started with the national idea that a code of crimi-nal procedure is supposed to be drafted not by judges but by parliament, by the legislators. To my mind that was short-sighted. They had the wrong im-pression of why we needed to redraft or amend our rules of procedure and evidence. We were the first court, opening the way. The draftsmen of the Rome Statute during the negotiating process simply did not trust judges.

I was told there was also this fear of the 'Cassese approach', namely judges overdoing it, becoming dangerous by, say, producing judgments that can be innovative. For example, at the ICTY, we said for the first time that war crimes could also be committed in internal armed conflicts. This was breaking new ground. You go beyond the black letter of the law because you look at the spirit of law.

Q: Do you have more examples of the 'Cassese approach'?

C: In January 1995, I pushed all the judges in the ICTY, saying, we cannot go on confirming indictments against people like Nikolic, or trying suspects like Tadic, these low-level alleged criminals. We have been set up at the expense of the international community, we have an important task, and so we have to go after the leaders. But when I summoned Richard Goldstone, the prosecutor, to a plenary meeting of the judges, he came with four people, including the chief of investigations and chief of prosecutions, and he set out his 'pyramidal vision' of criminal strategy. I asked how he intended to go about this? It's a pyramidal strategy, he said, we start at the bottom and go up to the summit. I said, it will take you twenty years to get to the leaders, Karadzic, Mladic, Milosevic and so on. Can we wait twenty years? This was also what Louise Arbour hinted at when she said that I should have been a prosecutor and not a judge.

So therefore in late January of 1995, there was a stormy meeting of the tribunal judges. I pushed my colleagues and was supported by some who shared the feeling that we should go after the leaders. But other colleagues did not consider it our job as judges; we simply had to wait for indictments and not impose a strategy on the prosecutor. But as the president I had to try to push for the notion behind this international tribunal. This tribunal had to be selective. Once I asked Goldstone how many people he thought had committed crimes in the former Yugoslavia. He said about 200,000 people. And I said, all right, so we cannot try 200,000 people. We can try only maybe 100. And these 100 must not be people like Tadic or Nikolic.

So then we had that stormy session of the judges. At the end of the session, we adopted a resolution where we set out in cautious terms, since the Security Council in its May 1993 resolution spoke of the great criminals, our deep concern about the prosecutorial strategy. When we were about to adopt this resolution, I said I had a moral duty toward Richard Goldstone to show him this draft resolution. We didn't mention him, but it was very clear that it was totally against his prosecutorial strategy. So I felt obliged to go and talk to him. He read the proposal, became terribly pale and said: 'You are fighting me, I will fight back, and you will see what I will do.' He was terribly upset and rightly so.

However, shortly before we were to resume the meeting of the judges, Goldstone came to my office with two people and said, 'Well, on reflection, if you change a few words I could even go ahead and subscribe to this resolution.'

And here I saw the clever politician. A fight would have meant going before the Security Council, before the Secretary-General, and he knew that we were supported by Boutros-Ghali and that it would be painful. He was extremely wise and politically savvy, understanding that he could negotiate. So I took out the poison, and we made some changes.

Q: Were these crucial changes?

C: No, but of course we toned down the whole spirit of the resolution. It was no longer aggressive, and in the end we issued a joint statement, a press release, indicating that the prosecutor shared our concern. This was on the 1st of February 1995. Five months later he issued the indictments for Sarajevo of Radovan Karadzic and Ratko Mladic, the civilian and military leader of the Bosnian Serbs, respectively. They were confirmed in July 1995.

The President as Father Figure

Q: The public face of the tribunal, and of the ICC today, has been the prosecutor. When Carla del Ponte left as chief prosecutor after eight years, the media reacted as if the tribunal was closing shop.

C: The prosecutor has to feed the judges by giving them indictments and can be aggressive, can afford to talk to the media, whereas the judges have to be reserved. Except for the president, who has to be a driving force, which has not been the case at every tribunal and seems to be lacking at the ICC, too.

Once in New York, when I was appointed as a monitor for the Special Court of Sierra Leone, I spoke to an American lady who had been in the office of the prosecutor in Sierra Leone and had resigned within two years. I asked her why she had resigned, and she said: 'What we missed in the Special Court for Sierra Leone was a sort of father figure, a leader, as you had been in the ICTY. Somebody who can be there from the outset, whereas in our case, the president had never been in Freetown.' And she was right. The judges would elect the president of the Sierra Leone court and then he could go back to London or Sri Lanka and communicate by fax or email. Ridiculous! You have to be there! Everybody must see you working there every day and being concerned and preoccupied, talking to the diplomats, going to see ambassadors, going to the UN.

Q: You say the ICC was lacking a father figure?

C: The first ICC president, Philippe Kirsch, is an excellent diplomat and lawyer. He has been extremely cautious. When you are at the top, you are overwhelmed by a lot of problems, including minor ones (for example, you have to confront judges who take too many holidays, stay away from The Hague for the wrong reasons, and so on. You cannot please them all). At the ICTY I had a fight with one of my best friends, an outstanding judge. He said that it should be acceptable for ICTY judges to sit on arbitrations. The judges of the International Court of Justice do, so why couldn't we do the same? But I wouldn't allow it. He had two arbitrations scheduled, and he also wanted to stay home and teach. However, I told him that he had a full salary as an international judge and could not stay at home and come only to The Hague for the plenary meetings of the judges and on top of that also sit on arbitrations.

Q: So did he resign?

C: Yes, he resigned.

Political Influence; Indicting Presidents: the ICTY and Milosevic of Yugoslavia, the ICC and Al-Bashir of Sudan

Q: Recently, Richard Goldstone mentioned during a lecture in The Hague that when he had indicted Karadzic and Mladic in 1995, the then Secretary-General of the UN, Boutros Boutros-Ghali said; 'How dare you indict Karadzic without consulting me?' And when the ICTY prosecutor said that the statute of the tribunal forbade him taking orders, the Secretary-General said: 'That's why I could not come to you, you should have come to me.' Was this out of concern about the peace process in Bosnia or for fear that Karadzic, as former president of Republika Srpska, would become an example of what could happen in the future to leaders, of the United States for instance?

C: No, I don't think that there was ever such a fear in states because of the limited scope of the ICTY jurisdiction. They knew that this matter only related to the leaders or culprits in a case relating to the former Yugoslavia.

Q: Yes, of course, the ICTY had no consequences for the Americans. But maybe you underestimate the political sense of the Americans. In the program in honor of the Praemium Erasmianum, which you and Benjamin Ferencz will receive this year, a film about the Nuremburg trial will be shown, made by Stuart and Budd Schulberg. They also made the long documentary film *The Nazi Plan* that was shown in the courtroom during the Nuremberg trials. When the film about the Nazi tribunal was finished in 1948, with images and sounds from the court in Nuremberg, it was put in a drawer because the Americans suppressed it. The Americans were too aware that this time there were German leaders in the dock, but that next time it could be a case against Americans.

C: This was because of the Cold War. Whereas in our case I don't think there was any political concern. Well, of course, I may have been totally unaware of political realities also because I was so concentrated on cases or judicial action. Goldstone probably had a better feeling. I only remember that Louise Arbour told me that after producing the indictment against President Milosevic, she on purpose first prepared the indictment, signed it and then told the great powers.

Q: She told the Dutch foreign minister and asked him to notify the foreign ministers in some other capitals, including Washington.

C: Only afterwards, because she feared she would be stopped by a few countries.

Sealed Indictments; Immunities

Q: Indictments against the major suspects could have come sooner.

C: Of course. When Louise Arbour became chief prosecutor, she withdrew a number of indictments against low-ranking offenders and introduced the practice of sealed indictments. At first, I was critical, because I felt that secret indictments were against the rights of the accused, but she proved me wrong.

She argued that this was the only way of being effective and that it was not necessarily a right of an accused to know immediately that he was being charged with an international crime.

Q: In the case of the ICC, specifically in the case of the Sudanese president Al-Bashir, you have said that it would have been more effective, more politically appropriate, to have issued a sealed arrest warrant. But some countries have made it known through back channels that they would not want to be in the position of suddenly having to serve a sealed arrest warrant on a high official. Let us look back. Charles Taylor was indicted under seal in March 2003, while he was president of Liberia. The following June, on his first trip outside Liberia, he went to a summit in Ghana, where the indictment was promptly announced. The Ghanaians were outraged because they were caught off guard. They later said they didn't have the machinery in place, did not know how to act. Charles Taylor then had the time to storm out of the country.

C: I believe there is a legal obligation to arrest somebody even if he is a head of state when he is on your territory. Let's be clear, either there is an obligation to arrest or there is no obligation. If there is no obligation, it makes no difference whether an arrest warrant or indictment is made public or not. So even with the public warrant like the one produced by ICC prosecutor Moreno-Ocampo, signed by the judges, the Sudanese president would not be arrested because in this case there's no obligation. Sudan is not a contracting party to the ICC. Immunities are lifted only in relation to member states.

The countries, in drafting the Statute, wanted to be careful not to infringe on sovereign rights of third countries. So, unless the Security Council stated, when referring the situation to the ICC, that not only Sudan but also *all* the UN member states were legally bound to comply, there would be no universal obligation. If Al-Bashir travels to Berlin, it is my view that the Berlin authorities may not arrest him because he says, 'Look, I am head of state and under your own Statute (Article 98 paragraph 2) you have to request the consent of my country, and since I represent my country, I tell you that I will never consent to my arrest.'

The ICJ in the *Arrest Warrant* case said that some state officials, in particular, foreign ministers, heads of states and of course prime ministers, enjoy *personal* (as opposed to functional) immunities. This means that once you step down as foreign minister or head of state you do not enjoy those immunities any longer, for they are linked to and conditional on your having a particular job. The ICJ said that the *functional* immunity (that is the immunity to which you are entitled because you are acting as a state official, an immunity that covers your actions even after leaving office) falls away only if the person acted 'in a private capacity' (*à titre privé*). However, whenever a defense minister, a foreign minister or a head of state orders, plans or willingly condones torture, he may not be considered as acting in his private capacity. He has indeed used all his state powers to order or plan or acquiesce in torture! He should therefore be held accountable and may not argue that he was acting as a state official and therefore was covered by functional immunity, with the consequence that only the *state* to which he belongs could incur international responsibility.

The House of Lords said that ordering torture does not belong to the function of a head of state or a prime minister and must therefore be a private act. Why not? This is what Mugabe does everyday, using and abusing his powers as head of state.

My view is that Al-Bashir, since he is a sitting head of state, enjoys personal immunities, not functional immunities. Why? Because he has to be protected by international law for the purpose of discharging his role in international dealings as head of state.

Q: Then how can you arrest him?

C: That's why I think you can't arrest him.

Prosecutorial Policy at the ICC

Q: Do you consider it a mistake that the ICC prosecutor went after the head of state of Sudan?

C: Even if legally possible, it would be politically impossible to arrest the sitting president of Sudan or any other country. The ICC blundered by issuing first an indictment to some minor people and then going after the head of state. As a result, he will not be arrested and has actually collected a lot of political support in Africa. There is a deadlock.

Several ICC judges are very concerned about the prosecution policy. Some countries are as well. They talk about the amount of money that is being spent. However, what is really regrettable is that so far, to the best of my knowledge, the prosecutor has never used his huge power to initiate investigations on his own accord. This is the one huge novelty of the Rome Statute. The trigger mechanisms are ridiculous because the states will never trigger any action against state officials of another state. And the Security Council may never take action again. What happened with Darfur was perhaps the one exception.

But instead of using his power to investigate and prosecute *proprio motu*, the prosecutor has played politics. For instance, when the Palestinian delegation said it wanted to recognize the ICC jurisdiction on an ad hoc basis after the attack on Gaza. The prosecutor did not dismiss the Palestinian initiative because this served as a message to please the Arab countries and to show that he was not only pursuing Africans. It would have been better to have informed the Palestinians right away that there was no jurisdiction because they are not a sovereign state. An immediate and blunt rejection is far less painful in the end. Instead, he said, 'This is very interesting, I will take it in to account.' So the Arab countries were happy.

Q: Could it possibly avoid being a political football?

C: Yes, of course. It takes integrity and judicial experience for a judge or a prosecutor to stay out of politics.

Q: That is what you have experienced at the ICTY.

C: Yes. The presidents there have not played political games, and that's why they are respected.

Q: The ICTY is a relatively small court covering one region, and it was established for a limited period of time. The ICC is playing the world stage. It is not inevitable that it becomes politicized?

C: No, not if you start gradually and don't concentrate on one area of the world only.

Q: The prosecutor says that the African cases were self referred and that is the best that can happen, because you are then ensured of the cooperation of the referring state.

C: It is the wrong path to go for self-referral by a government instead of taking the initiative yourself. The self-referrals are always against rebels or other enemies of the government. So why not pick up a case in Latin America? And start working on Afghanistan. Why is the ICC so terribly afraid of Afghanistan? It is a member state of the ICC. Therefore, all international crimes committed on its territory, whoever the author, come under the ICC jurisdiction.

International Criminal Law Instrumentalized; Its Limitations and Relation to Human Rights

Q: Despite the difficulties, it appears that international criminal law has become an instrument of the international human rights system. Because political reactions have been weak or opportunistic in the face of massive state crimes, the tendency now is to fall back on criminal law. Either humanitarian intervention, or international criminal law. You have said that you consider the principle of international criminal prosecution to be an effective response.

C: Yes, because you strike at the very heart of the problem, which is not the state. Holding states accountable is what the European Court of Human Rights or the Inter-American Court of Human Rights can do. They find that Russia is in breach of say Article 2 or 3 of the European Convention because of their atrocities in Chechnya, and then the courts demand that Russia pay €20,000 to the Chechnyan victims. Is it enough? No, it's not enough! But the people who were killing in Chechnya – or in Turkey or in Italy or anywhere – are scot-free, they are not punished. The police or military officers who committed the crimes will keep their jobs. For Russia, it's peanuts to pay €20,000 every few months to the victims, namely to those individuals who have suffered from serious violations of the European Convention on Human Rights. So this is not the solution. The solution is to say we will now start punishing the Minister of Defense, the police officers who torture and kill, the military people who use helicopters to kill civilians. The existing international bodies are important, but they don't achieve much. The international community is totally impotent vis-à-vis say Myanmar, China, Zimbabwe, and other countries where the whole state is repressive, authoritarian. And the international community is absolutely impotent against North Korea while it represses and starves its own population. So, therefore, if the international community has no effective response against massive violations of human rights, why not use criminal repression as a tool?

But of course, a response through criminal law has many limitations. You act only after the violations have occurred. And you can only hope that this will have a deterrent effect. It sends a strong message however. If you inculcate the notion that a Minister of Defense, even if he's a us citizen, could be punished one day, he might think twice about saying torture is legal. The message is, even Mr. Rumsfeld can be brought to court. Maybe not in the us, but perhaps if he goes abroad.

True, criminal justice may be dispensed by international tribunals with all their limitations, particularly the icc. The icc is proving to be weak, and this is indeed disappointing. But one day it could become a very effective body. National courts can play an important role, exercising universal jurisdiction, but within limits. They cannot sit in judgment on gross breaches of human rights, on international crimes everywhere. A Spanish judge cannot handle all the crimes committed in Africa, in Latin America, in some European countries and so on. I gather that Spain, like Belgium, is narrowing the scope of its law. It will require a nexus between the crime and the state. In most countries, you can start investigations, but you can move to trial only if the accused is present on the territory of that state.

The Crime of Aggression

Q: Next year the member states of the icc have to decide whether the court should have jurisdiction over crimes of aggression. What do you expect to happen?

C: I very much doubt that the crime of aggression will be accepted as a crime in the Rome Statute in 2010. The major powers will not agree on a written definition of aggression, because that would mean defining self-defense. Self-defense has been left undefined until now on purpose. There is some sort of agreement on the distinction between pre-emptive and preventive self-defense. Preventive or anticipatory self-defense means that a state uses force against an attack or an imminent threat, including by a non-state entity like a group of terrorists. There seems to be agreement that this falls within lawful self-defense. But things are different when there is no imminent threat. A government knows that, for instance, a neighboring country is building a nuclear reactor, which will start operating in one year, and it decides to go there and destroy the reactor. Recent UN documents consider this kind of pre-emptive self-defense unlawful, and I agree, but that is a minority opinion. It does not necessarily reflect the opinion of the major powers. As a result, they don't want to define the crime of aggression, because then they would have to take a clear stand on this category of self-defense. Take the attack on Iraq. There was only one European international lawyer who argued that it was lawful, and this was a distinguished British judge. The Americans and the British foreign office claimed that it was lawful. If you define a massive armed attack like this as unlawful, you should say it is aggression. This also makes it easier to define the crime of aggression. Then it is not only a breach of international law, but also of international criminal law, implying that you have criminal responsibility.

Q: Do you want the crime of aggression to be included in the Statute of the ICC?

C: I hope that sooner or later it will be part of the Statute. But my point is that it is already a crime under customary international law. You cannot write off so many judgments, in Nuremberg, in Tokyo and the recent judgment by the British House of Lords on 29 March 2006. The latter delivered an important decision in international law when it declared that the crime of aggression is a crime under customary international law, yet not a criminal offence under English law. The 20 appellants, in *R. v. Jones et al*, had been either charged or convicted in different proceedings for causing criminal damage and/or committing aggravated trespass on UK military bases during protests against the then imminent military attack of Iraq by the Coalition forces. In their defense, the appellants argued that they had used reasonable force to prevent a crime – the crime of aggression against Iraq – and that, therefore, their actions were justified. The thrust of their argument was that an attack on Iraq would amount to an unlawful war of aggression. Hence they were entitled to take measures aimed at preventing it.

However, there is a grey area, also when we say that aggression is prohibited in customary law. To my mind the pre-emptive attacks are prohibited. You cannot attack Iraq in a massive way if there is no previous armed attack or imminent armed attack by Iraq against other countries. If Israel today attacks Iran or Syria to destroy a nuclear reactor or others arms of mass destruction, this would be an act of aggression. However, this is an isolated view, not covered by a general consensus in the international community and thus remains a grey area. It has been left undefined on purpose by the major powers. When there is a clear act of aggression, as in the attack by Iraq against Kuwait, there is a dual regime of responsibility, not only the state responsibility, but also criminal liability of Saddam Hussein and his bunch of leaders of Iraq.

I need to separate state responsibility from criminal liability because to hold Saddam Hussein as a leader liable for the crime of aggression, you need more elements, both objective and subjective, including the *mens rea*, a special intent (*dolus specialis*), for instance to appropriate a foreign territory, or to topple the government wielding power there, or to gain control over the natural resources existing there. In other words, the aggressor state uses force because it clearly intends to obtain economic advantages, or to interfere in the internal affairs of another state by toppling the government, or to bring about political or ideological change.

Q: Would the criminal intent be difficult to prove?

C: No. If you say: you invaded Kuwait to get its oil, you have the *mens rea* to occupy the country to control its resources.

Q: Here you have an overlap between the head of state and the person who is individually responsible.

C: That is why the Allies rightly imposed a dual regime. They held the leaders individually criminally responsible in Nuremberg, and they held the whole German state responsible for breaching international law (the bilateral or multilateral treaties to which Germany was a party, as well as the international customary rules prohibiting states from engaging in war as an instrument of national policy, rules that had evolved from the Paris Pact of 1928). The whole country was held responsible and had to pay damages.

Q: How would it work in practice, if the ICC could prosecute for aggression?

C: The finding of aggression by the Security Council, a political body, and the finding of aggression by a judicial body should remain completely independent. Of course, if the Security Council determined that a state had committed an act of aggression against another state, it would be much easier for the ICC prosecutor to conclude the same.

But whatever the Security Council decides is not binding on the prosecutor, though it will make his finding easier. On the other hand, it would be very awkward for the Security Council if the prosecutor reached the opposite conclusion. There are, however, possibilities of inconsistencies. Why? The Security Council is not making a finding on a breach of criminal law, but of the UN Charter. There the threshold is lower. For instance, the fact that an aircraft invades the airspace of a sovereign country is a violation of the territorial integrity of another country, but this is not an act of aggression. An act of aggression is much more than a group of soldiers driving tanks into a neighboring country or crazy soldiers firing at soldiers of another country. In such cases you have a breach of international law with state responsibility. They may lead to diplomatic solutions, or the payment of damages. But a massive invasion by troops on a large scale and over a few days of the territory of another country could amount to an act of aggression. The Security Council could say under Article 39 of the UN Charter that this is an act of aggression, but the prosecutor may decide not to step in. The Security Council as a political body is only interested in putting an end to a breach of the peace, not in identifying individual perpetrators. The prosecutor needs many more elements. A massive attack on the territory of another state could last two days in response to sporadic attacks. This disproportionate response is a breach of international law; it is an act of aggression because there is no authorization by the Security Council. Probably, it is not self-defense because there is a lack of proportionality. But since they withdrew, they showed there is a lack of intent to occupy the country, to topple the government or permanently control the national resources. People don't understand that aggression can be a serious breach of international law (entailing state responsibility) as well as an international crime (entailing individual criminal liability), but not necessarily both.

Q: And when the prosecutor says, 'This is a crime of aggression,' the Security Council does not have to agree?

C: It does not. It may be politically expedient to disagree with the prosecutor. The Security Council may not want to set a precedent or is afraid the country might overreact once its use of force is labeled aggression. I can understand that. The Security Council has to take into account so many elements that have nothing to do with legal considerations. Its purpose is to seek or maintain peace. It can give a private, undisclosed warning, however, telling the state it has been an aggressor and must stop, although that will not be expressed publicly.

Tensions between Criminal Law and International Law; nullum Crimen Principle; back to Röling

Q: Former ICTY chief prosecutor Louise Arbour wrote in your book, *The Humanitarian dimension of international law, Selected papers*: 'The great divide, exemplified by the profound intellectual tensions between Cassese and me, came from our background in international and criminal law, respectively. ... Criminal law is authoritative, rule-based, rigorous, and designed in part to keep in check the immense powers of the states. ... International law is consensual, norm-based, fluid, and immensely deferential to states.'

C: Louise Arbour is right to some extent, but she is also wrong. Like many national criminal lawyers, she tends to transpose domestic notions of criminal law onto the international level. That's why for instance now, in Europe, not so much in the US, there is a big intellectual fight between national criminal lawyers who feel that international criminal lawyers like myself tend not to be rigorous enough. They think that we are expanding basic concepts of criminal law, making them too hazy and vague, whereas criminal law should be strict. That's why these lawyers want to re-appropriate this area.

In the early 19th century, the German criminal lawyer Feuerbach was the first to theorize the *nullum crimen sine lege* principle. You cannot be punished for any conduct unless that conduct was labeled as criminal before you engaged in it. This principle is a way of limiting the omnipotence of the state, of the executive. I often quote Franz von Liszt, who wrote in 1893 that these principles are 'the bulwark of the citizen against the state's omnipotence; they protect the individual against the ruthless power of the majority, against the Leviathan. However paradoxical it may sound, the Criminal Code is the criminal's Magna Charta – *Magna Charta des Verbrechers'*.

Q: Why should that be different in international criminal law? In Nuremberg and Tokyo the leaders were tried without prior written criminal laws prohibiting the crimes with which the suspects were charged. In your conversations with Bert Röling, he said that one of the possible negative results of the Nuremberg and Tokyo rulings could be that the victor of the next war could now say that he was entitled to make new laws and then punish those who have breached them.

C: Röling himself provided the best response. He accepted the fact that the crime against the peace as charged in Nuremberg and Tokyo was retroactive law. He said in his dissenting opinion in the Tokyo Judgment that in international law, the word 'crime' is applied to concepts with different meanings. It can indicate acts comparable to political crimes in domestic law. The decisive element is *danger* rather than *guilt*. The criminal is more *enemy* than *villain*, and punishment reflects a necessary *political measure* rather than *retribution*. I think this conceptual approach was very good. He was aware that you could not automatically, mechanically, transpose principles of law from a national setting, where you have that great progress of civilization, the division of powers, advocated by Montesquieu, to the international level. However, Röling added that since the authors of such crimes are considered enemies, their punishment is more in the nature of a political measure than judicial retribution. It followed that in his view, if found guilty, they were not to be hanged.

Q: You could argue that because in international law there is no counterbalance, no proper *trias politica*, we should be extra careful, we should have an even more rigorous rule-based international criminal law system to protect individuals against this amorphous body of human rights lawyers, international humanitarian experts, criminal lawyers who get together and think this is good enough.

C: In Nuremberg there was a very clear notion with regard to crimes against humanity. Of course there were no laws prohibiting crimes against humanity, no law prohibiting persecution, no law prohibiting euthanasia. However, the mass persecution and the mass killing, the extermination by the Germans of the Jews only because they were Jewish, of Gypsies only because they were Gypsies, basically were killing and murder: crimes clearly prohibited in national criminal law. So even if it was not a crime provided for in international law, everybody knew this was forbidden. The Nazis were well aware that what they did was criminal. Why else were they keeping Auschwitz, Mauthausen, all the concentration camps secret?

Q: The criticism of national criminal lawyers is not only aimed at the codification of international crimes after the fact. There are also the procedural and evidentiary rules of criminal law meant to protect the individual against the state. Isn't that also what Arbour was talking about? In international humanitarian law and human rights law, the criminal law system is watered down to suit political interests, the interests of states.

C: What Arbour probably meant was: Cassese argues in the *Tadic* decision in 1995 at the ICTY for the first time that rape in internal armed conflict is as much a war crime as in international war conflict. That was against the *nullum crimen* principle. Rape was only regarded as a national offense, so punishable under Serbian law or Bosnian law, not under international law. And I said, sorry, I don't understand why we should not go beyond this very strict, formalistic, rigorous approach taken in international law. And this actually was nothing new. One of the cases, which I dug up, a Belgian court-martial case, *Auditeur militaire v. K.V*, of 1950 is an instructive indication of 'judicial creativity'. The defendant, a German officer, had been accused of torturing and inflicting cruel treatment on civilians in occupied Belgium. In particular, he had repeatedly delivered severe blows to the faces of civilians. The Court noted that Article 46 of the Regulations, annexed to the Fourth Hague Convention of 1907, loosely banned attacks on 'family honor and rights, the lives of persons and private property as well as religious convictions'. It banned attacks on life and honor, not on the body as such. The relevant rules, thus, did not expressly prohibit violence or ill treatment against the inhabitants of occupied countries. Nevertheless, the Court held that, on the strength of the famous *Martens* clause, it had to look for principles of international law derived from the laws of humanity and the dictates of the public conscience. To this effect, it cited Article 5 of the Universal Declaration of Human Rights as evidence that inflicting cruel treatment on civilians was considered prohibited. It consequently held that the accused was guilty of the crimes with which he had been charged.

The body of international law is made up of a set of rules that gradually emerge, and they may also evolve as a result of the impact of the common conscience of mankind on customary international law. Should they have said that the German officer, when he was beating up those people, knew that he was not breaching international law because international law only prohibited attacks on life and honor? I agree with the Belgian court.

Röling was so good also because his legal construct was logical, clear cut and coherent. The Nuremberg judges wrongly said that the crime of aggression was already part of customary international law. But Röling acknowledged that the crime of aggression was not prohibited, legally speaking, and in this respect Nuremberg was wrong. He said that it was very important, nevertheless, to punish those people because they had committed a political offense.

The Supreme Court of Israel set an example of a logical and intelligent approach in the *Eichmann* case, when it dealt with crimes against humanity. It produced a wonderful judgment where you have this step-by-step argument. So, argument number one: those crimes were already prohibited by customary international law when Eichmann engaged them. Two: even assuming they were not prohibited, it would be legitimate to punish Eichmann for those crimes, because the *nullum crimen sine lege* principle was not a binding rule of customary law, and therefore retroactive punishment is admissible; third, even if 'the sense of justice generally recoils' from retroactive punishment, in the case of such odious crimes as those committed by Eichmann, 'one's sense of justice must necessarily recoil even more from the non-punishment of the persons who participated in such outrages'.

Q: Does this reasoning still hold for the international tribunals and the ICC?

C: No, because by now, the *nullum crimen* principle is well settled in international law, except of course for the crime of aggression because of the political problems with aggression. Slowly, a system of strict legality has developed. It has been made possible by the many treaties, like the Torture Convention and ultimately in the statutes of the ad hoc tribunals and the ICC. The ICC Statute says in Article 22: 'A person shall not be criminally responsible under this Statute unless the conduct in question constitutes, at the time it takes place, a crime within the jurisdiction of the Court.'

Q.: How do you react to Arbour's remark that international law is more deferential to States? That is harsh criticism. Could you say that international law is more vulnerable to politicization?

C: Louise Arbour is right. I stressed the same concept in my book on *International Criminal Law* (2nd edition, pp. 8-9), where I tried to emphasize that while international criminal law addresses itself to individuals and must of necessity be strict and strictly interpreted because of its repressive and punitive nature, the whole body of public international law addresses itself to sovereign states with a view to reconciling their conflicting exigencies; as a result, there the *normative* role of law is more important than its *repressive* function.

The ICC Statute as New International Criminal Code; the End of Fragmentation?

Q: Has the Statute of Rome of the ICC established a new standard, a criminal code for all international criminal law?

C: Not at all. Unfortunately, the German, Dutch, Spanish and Italian criminal lawyers, being used to studying and commenting on written criminal codes, tend to take a small piece of international law, namely the ICC Statute, and project this onto the international level. They think that the whole body of international criminal law consists of the twenty substantive articles of the ICC Statute. I keep telling them that the ICC Statute only applies to the ICC!

The ICC Statute departs from customary international law in many respects, and in particular on the issue of superior orders. In Nuremberg and Tokyo and later at the ICTY and ICTR, it was established that there is no room for the defense of superior orders. An accused person cannot be relieved of his or her criminal responsibility by claiming that he was acting pursuant to an order of a superior. In the ICC Statute, by contrast, when an accused is charged with war crimes, the defense of superior orders is made possible. Only in the case of war crimes. Why, would you ask, does the Rome Statute deviate from the law established in Nuremberg and upheld since then by the international tribunals? Well, the Americans and the Israelis have pushed to admit the defense of superior orders in war crimes cases because they could very well imagine themselves one day being called before the Court for war crimes. As a compromise, they discarded any defense of superior orders in case of genocide and crimes against humanity. This is a totally silly distinction. The ICC Statute supposes that a soldier, while fighting, would be aware of the difference between his acts as war crimes or as crimes against humanity and would realize that crimes against humanity – or his taking part in a genocide – are manifestly criminal, while his war crimes could be legitimized by orders from his commander. Too often an act can be defined as a war crime and a crime against humanity at the same time, so how could a soldier in full action distinguish between the two?

If you go to the ICTY, or to any international tribunal, we are not bound by the ICC definition of superior order, of mistake of law, of mistake of fact or their strict definition of command responsibility and so on. We can, of course, take the ICC Statute into account, for instance here at the Special

Tribunal for Lebanon and, of course, as an interesting piece of international legislation. But we are not bound by it as customary international law.

Q: If the ICC Statute only applies to the ICC as you say, and other courts can interpret international criminal law as they go along, isn't there a risk of fragmentation, different courts with different definitions of crimes and different interpretations of basic notions of law? A flaw in the requirement of clear labeling?

C: International criminal law consists of two big bodies. You have customary international law, which is applicable to the whole world, and then you have the statutes of the individual tribunals and courts. The statute of a particular tribunal may depart from customary international law.

Therefore, some fragmentation may emerge, although the existence of a core of fundamental principles of criminal law should confer some unity on the whole corpus of international criminal law.

Q: The drafters also added the excuse of self-defense to the Statute, not only the age-old right of a person to defend himself or herself against an imminent threat or attack, but a much wider notion of self-defense. How and why did this come to pass in Rome?

C: If you want to avert a crime against other people, this can be acceptable as self-defense. But can the use of force to avert a crime against any asset that is useful for war purposes be considered self-defense? For instance, when you kill a lot of people (say, enemy combatants that you kill by using prohibited weapons, thereby committing what would amount to a war crime) because you want to save an ammunition depot? It is totally absurd to call that self-defense. So, here is an example of why it is a good thing that other courts are not bound by these rules that have become part of the ICC Statute for reasons of political self-interest. To me it is clear that in international criminal law, self-defense can act as a justification (that is, a circumstance relieving you of responsibility for a crime you may have committed) only if you intend to protect your own life and limb or the life and limb of another person from an imminent or actual unlawful attack. But self-defense cannot be invoked to protect property. Otherwise, with a view to saving a military compound containing food, water and other supplies indispensable to the survival of the servicemen from an impending unlawful enemy attack, an officer would be allowed to order the launch of an indiscriminate attack against the enemy combatants and the civilian population. This would be absurd indeed.

New Methods of War, New Laws of Warfare?

Q: Since the laws of war were born during an era when military forces confronting each other were entitled to diminish the military power of the opponent, the question obviously arises: are the laws of warfare adequate as the wars have changed? In contemporary wars, both the victims and the perpetrators are often mainly civilians. In Iraq alone, half of the American forces consisted of civilians working among others for private military corporations, for instance. Non-state actors take part in wars in Africa, in the Middle East and in terrorism. Wars change, should the laws of warfare change with them?

C: We would need to modernize and update what we call the international humanitarian law of armed conflict, the laws of warfare. Why? Let me say a few obvious things. You know there are two notions of war. One going back to Jean-Jacques Rousseau, who said war is a confrontation between two armies, which of course comply with their set of rules, have to conduct their warfare in a dignified manner and fight each other as soldiers, not as citizens. Therefore, the fight must be between combatants, and the civilians must be kept out of any fight. And then you have the new vision of war applied for the first time by Napoleon in the Napoleonic Wars, and then theorized by von Clausewitz in his very lengthy and boring but extremely intelligent book. They saw wars involving the whole population. In his notion of total warfare, all-out war, you can't distinguish between a soldier and a citizen. Every citizen is a soldier. Now the whole set of international humanitarian law is rightly based on the notion of Rousseau that you have to constantly bear in mind that a distinction must be made between civilians and combatants, in an attempt to minimize the suffering of the civilians. However, most contemporary wars are asymmetric, because you have a big power against groups of rebels, terrorists or other non-state actors, often in possession of light weapons only, or missile launchers. And often they don't have much training, they have no barracks, they live everywhere, they hide everywhere. They can use booby traps and roadside bombs to try to blow up the tanks of the enemy. So, therefore, those people are normally hiding among the civilians. We know that Hezbollah, in Lebanon in 2006, would bring a pick-up truck to a square, or to a road full of civilians, launch ten missiles against Israel, and then move away quickly. Israel retaliated and hit all those civilians who had nothing to do with Hezbollah. Those conflicts are chaos.

That's why I asked myself many times whether we should update the two Additional Protocols to the Geneva Conventions, regulating international and non-international armed conflicts, respectively. However, there is very little interest because the terrorists and rebel groups would never take part in the drafting of new conventions. Most are not even liberation movements. In Geneva, when we drafted the Geneva Protocols in the 1970s, at least the PLO was there. But states are not that interested either. They don't want to limit their own power. Drafting new rules of warfare would come to nothing. Imagine that the state powers would have to first of all take on all the interests and concerns of the non-state entities. They will never do so because they consider these groups as terrorists who simply must be killed. The same way most states in the 19th and 20th centuries used to think of rebels. Rebels are people who must be hanged. You capture them, and you hang them. They have no rights. So, therefore, now the same applies to terrorists, I mean the Hezbollah, the Taliban, and so on, they must simply be liquidated. Why should the contracting states impose self-limitations? On a few occasions, I floated a set of proposals, but I saw, even in Geneva, that there's no hope that the rules will be adapted to modern warfare. I spoke in Israel with leading people in the IDF, the Israeli Defense Force. These are members of the Israeli army with very good legal training. We had an informal discussion lasting an entire afternoon, but they flat out told me that what I proposed was not workable and would in the end impose serious limitations on any professional army.

Q: So that's the end of that?

C: Since there's no hope of drafting a new treaty or set of conventions or set of international binding rules, we could at least go for a set of guidelines. The International Committee of the Red Cross could work out a set of authoritative guidelines, which would be presented to states and non-state entities alike as reference points.

Q: Could you give an example?

C: Say, a definition or description of precautions to be taken before launching an attack. Any belligerent is obliged to take precautions to make sure that civilians are not attacked. But the rule is very general and far from concrete. Take Israel – if you talk to the Israelis they say that they phoned all the mobile phones in southern Lebanon or that they dropped leaflets to warn civilians of an attack as they said they did recently in Gaza. Or they say they warned civilians through loudspeakers. The Russians will tell you, that in Chechnya, they went around with huge helicopters with loudspeakers and warned the population: leave the area because we are about to launch an attack. And in the case of *Isayeva, Yusupova and Bazayeav* v. *Russia* (judgment of 24 February 2005), the victims before the European Court of Human Rights said, well, we never heard anything because there was such a noise.

When you give detailed guidelines, setting out how precautions would be effective or how to apply the principle of proportionality in actual fact, there would be a basis to act upon. On many occasions I took as an example the excellent judgment by the Israeli Supreme Court in the targeted killings case, where its president Barack set out to give concrete examples of how you can apply proportionality. Judge Barack gave a methodology of how you can make an instrument out of a very big notion – proportionality – a tool for guiding the states. And we would also have to think of duties to be imposed upon say both military powers and non-state entities. Let them keep a record before and after any attack and let them, when a lot of civilians have been killed, automatically have the duty to make a finding of what happened. And let them pay! Let there be an obligation to pay the victims. Because they kill people, wound and maim people and don't pay one penny. Not one penny. Yes, the Americans paid the Chinese in Belgrade after bombing their embassy. But only because it was China, a powerful state. But, in general, we don't pay the poor Palestinians or the poor people in Afghanistan or the countless people being killed in Africa. They laugh at you if you say: why don't you institute criminal or civil proceedings? At least an internal inquiry could be initiated, with a report you make public. You honestly describe what occurred, whether there were serious armed attacks involving killing of civilians, to what extent the actions were justified and where they were disproportionate. But then in any case we pay the victims. Except when their own side misused the civilians, and there the civilians must know that we will not compensate them. This could be an incentive, a strong incentive for the civilians to find the courage to prevent, for instance, the Taliban hiding in their houses. They will not get any compensation if they did not try to distance themselves as much as possible from these bloody militants.

I know, international law must be made by dreamers. Look at Henri Dunant, he was an incompetent businessman and also a bit crazy, but he also was a visionary, and we owe it to him that the Red Cross was set up.

Q: True, true. On the other hand, exactly because wars became all-out wars, 'wars among the people' as General Rupert Smith calls them, there is also this feeling that law is too weak and too powerless. International law seems to be slowly losing territory again. After Nuremberg, the Geneva Conventions and many other treaties were established. There was this idea that law could get a hold on the violence of the world, but did it succeed?

C: Yes, although to a limited extent. On the other hand, some headway could be made. If we set in place a two-pronged approach, say a set of guidelines and also a monitoring mechanism, it could be possible to react almost instantaneously to the use of force. It should be a very small monitoring mechanism, very modest, with very neutral people of great integrity that everybody would respect. They would step in immediately and announce their arrival to the belligerents. They would say to the Americans and the Taliban: we want to come right away to be there, to watch what you are doing, and we will report to you confidentially. And then if you keep on killing and abusing the laws of war, we will make a public report, but we want to be there at the outset. And we are a very tiny group, just coming to watch.

There already is a Fact-Finding Commission, which is called the 'Sleeping Beauty'. It is a wonderful commission set up under Article 90 of the first Geneva Protocol in 1977. They meet twice a year in Geneva; there is a turnover of members of this Commission. They are very competent people, scholars, professors, NGO people, judges, criminal judges, and they are not being used by anybody. It's the Sleeping Beauty. Why? It was our fault, I was there, I was a member of the Italian delegation in Geneva. It was conceived as a sort of a quasi-judicial body. But in fact you need a very small body, which can act on short notice and step in. It should of course carry great moral authority, with very competent people, say Swiss or Swedes. Of course you would not send three Americans to an African conflict, you would send Africans. As soon as the conflict breaks out, they go there, and they announce it publicly. Who would oppose? Even Israel might not oppose if such a mechanism were set up, because it would react as an existing body, not established especially for this conflict, but instead treating all conflicts equally.

Q: So the fact-finding commission for the recent violence in Gaza, led by Richard Goldstone, is not what you propose. Goldstone said that the Israelis don't want him to interview victims in Gaza nor Israeli victims in the south of Israel.

C: That whole process was totally wrong. Because it started off in the Human Rights Council, which of course in the majority is already biased against Israel. Goldstone, who is an outstanding professional and a man of great integrity, said he would only take the job if he could investigate the use of force of both parties in the conflict. I hope that Israel will accept his role, given his moral authority. But if you have a pre-existing commission that can call on specialists in military affairs, humanitarian law, judges and doctors, no prior political discussion has to be held in a UN organ or commission. The team can just go.

Q: In *The Tokyo Trial and Beyond*, you discuss with Röling the theory of coercive warfare. It holds that war against civilians is less costly and more effective than war against the military forces of the opponent. By attacking the population, the government can be pressured to capitulate. So, instead of a basic notion that the suffering of civilians should be limited, civilians become the target. And in Afghanistan, in Iraq and in the former Yugoslavia to a lesser extent before that, the battle tactics almost totally depended on air support, which means that the killing of civilians has become part of the military policy. Both Human Rights Watch and Amnesty International have reported that the Israeli drones indiscriminately killed Palestinian civilians. Do you consider this the unavoidable effect of technology, which makes the distinction between civilians and combatants void? Or are the civilians purposefully targeted here? Or could you even say that when large-scale civilian casualties are unavoidable or 'coercive', this is equal to purposefully targeting civilians, these are 'fusillades'?

C: Yes, of course when an airman deliberately attacks civilians or willingly undertakes indiscriminate attacks by shelling areas where there are both enemy combatants and civilians, he commits a war crime. The airman is duty bound to refrain from any attack when his shelling is likely to indiscriminately kill civilians in addition to combatants.

However, I must add that to a large extent the killing of civilians is a sad consequence of both modern technology and the asymmetric nature of most conflicts. And it is also sad that no airman is ever prosecuted for indiscriminate killing. The fact nevertheless remains that when a belligerent attacks civilians, he eventually pays a heavy price, because the world public opinion reacts with outrage, and in addition the civilians who survive end up siding with their own combatants, and their hatred for the enemy increases. The belligerent attacking and killing enemy civilians may win the battle, but then has got to confront the indignation and the censure of foreign countries and public opinion, and the surge in animosity and will to fight back by the enemy civilians.

Q: Philosopher Avishai Margalit and social scientist Michael Walzer, the author of *Just and Unjust Wars*, published an article on 14 May 2009 about the distinction between combatants and civilians in reaction to the recent intervention by Israel in Gaza. Their conclusion is remarkable. 'This is the guideline we advocate: Conduct your war in the presence of non-combatants on the other side with the same care *as if* your citizens were the non-combatants.' Merely *not intending to kill* civilians is not enough; soldiers must *intend not to kill* civilians, Margalit and Walzer say. This is a far cry from the current practice in many armed conflicts.

C: The problem with this approach is that it boils down to a moral imperative, to an ethical tenet, which risks being ignored or downplayed by the military. I think it would be more realistic and effective to request that a belligerent (i) should always check ex post facto whether its troops went beyond what is prescribed by international humanitarian law and, if they did, should pay compensation to the victims, and (ii) should accept from the inception of their armed hostilities that a monitoring body will exercise its oversight. This twofold approach might discourage combatants from attacking civilians as much as possible.

Q: Should we forget about the separation between combatants or distinction between combatants and non-combatants?

C: I firmly believe that although it has become so complicated to make this distinction, we have to stick to it. Because if we drop even this distinction, we are lost. So, in spite of its weakness, in spite of it becoming so fuzzy and questionable, I think it is still crucial. However, it should be replaced as soon as possible by what I call the new guidelines, setting clearer standards. I remember I had a discussion with my Israeli friends about targeted killings. I prepared a legal opinion, at the request of Israeli lawyers acting for Palestinians, that was put before the Israeli Supreme Court. Judge Barack cited it many times, although he didn't share my view. I asked them the following question: take the case of a Palestinian leader, who is fighting against the occupying Israeli power, who prepares his attacks and goes home and has lunch with his wife and his children, or takes his children to the cinema in Ramallah. Can you kill him? Can you send a missile as you Israelis normally do? Do you kill him in a taxi while he's going to the cinema with his children? And they answered: yes, when he's at home, we don't know whether he's actually planning a new terrorist attack or whether he's sleeping. He is a military objective, and there is of course collateral damage, the poor lady and the poor children die. That's not our fault. He is an enemy; therefore he's a combatant.

I told them: not to my mind. Just as an Israeli general who goes to the synagogue to pray or, say, he goes to a movie with his family should not be attacked. Although he's a general and maybe a key leader and strategist of the Israeli army, at the moment he's praying at the synagogue or dining with his family, he cannot be a military objective. At that moment he's not a combatant.

Q: And the Ministry of Defense, for instance, where 500 people, also secretaries, kitchen personnel, are working?

C: A Ministry of Defense is a military objective.

Q: And if Bin Laden goes to visit his mother because she's on her deathbed?

C: But Bin Laden, I would say, is not a combatant or non-combatant, he's a terrorist. So, you try to arrest him, and if you can't arrest him, you kill him. He is not someone who is taking part in a combat. He is a leader of a terrorist organization, which cannot be equated to a non-state armed organization. He is simply a terrorist leader, and he falls under criminal law, not under international humanitarian law. Repressive or coercive action can be undertaken against him, which may be at odds with international humanitarian law. So there, I would say, yes, if you are absolutely unable to detain him, you wound or kill him, and you may perforce kill also his mother who is next to him.

That's why many Americans are wrong in over-using the label of terrorist. You lose sight of the real terrorists. I mean Bin Laden is always to be regarded as a terrorist, not as an enemy combatant. Whereas the Taliban fighting in Afghanistan or Pakistan or Hezbollah in southern Lebanon, they are combatants. To be sure, in combat they were using terrorist methods; a combatant can use terrorist methods, but this would amount to a war crime. Look at the Israelis who were fighting against the British, they were using terrorist methods as well.

Q: Do you agree that people working in the army are at a loss and would be helped by clear guidelines? Now they are fed with political – sometimes religious – incentives and propaganda, instead of professional instructions.

C: When I was in Darfur, I secretly met an officer of the Sudanese army, who was prepared to talk to me in confidence. He had been court-marshaled by his own army. I asked him why he was talking to me about the misdeeds of the Sudanese army, in particular about the attacks on villages in Darfur. He said: because I am a military man. I have been brought up and trained by the British. I am a man used to military discipline, and I can't stand the Janjaweed going out there, raping women and killing civilians. To me, it is against my dignity as a soldier.

Responsibility of States; Individual Criminality and System Criminality; back to Röling again

Q: Military academies all over the world are teaching international humanitarian law now. They are trying to help their soldiers. All their doctrines and teachings are contradicted by reality. But there is also backlash. The military and their political leaders too are anticipating criminal procedures and building barriers against them.

C: Let me remind you of the wonderful distinction made by Röling between *individual criminality* and *system criminality*. The soldiers are prepared to be prosecuted for what he called individual criminality. Rape, for instance, is against morality, against the rules of the army and against the dignity of the military man. But what about the system criminality, such as large-scale torture, mass killing of civilians, persecution of ethnic or religious groups? When, for instance, the Soviets got the message in 1945: you arrive in Berlin, you can rape all the women, because all these Germans are bastards. The massive violence by the Russians is system criminality. There, the rape is condoned and becomes a way of punishing the enemy. The torture, like in Guantanamo and so on, is also a manifestation of system criminality. I think this is a crucial distinction.

System criminality, as Röling correctly pointed out, will never be punished by the army itself, only by the enemy, if the latter won the war or, I would add, by an international criminal tribunal.

In Italy recently, there was a case against Italian soldiers who fired on an ambulance in Baghdad. They killed four women. The Italian military court in Rome has to prosecute – in Italy prosecution is compulsory. Because Italy is party to the ICC, it had to prosecute because otherwise the ICC could – in theory – have stepped in. Italy prosecuted. And then rules were produced to excuse the killing, to establish that this killing was not criminal conduct.

Still, I insist that it is very important for national courts to deal with war crimes. You cannot punish only the leaders and not the executioner. You have to punish the commander of Auschwitz, but also the Nazi guard who was taking part in the selection of people and in the cruelties and murders. There were so many ss criminals, in the camps and elsewhere, whom you cannot bring to trial before an international tribunal. There should be a scheme that lays the responsibility for the prosecution of the leaders with the international courts and the prosecution of the others (the executioners, the small fry) with the domestic criminal courts. That was the scheme that was outlined by that little appreciated genius, Murray C. Bernays. He studied at Harvard and Columbia, and as a colonel on the US Army's General Staff, he was the designer of the program to deal with the Nazi war criminals. He played a huge role at the outset. Initially, there was the Morgenthau plan, which called for the summary execution of the Nazi leaders. Roosevelt favored the Morgenthau approach, but when he died, Truman ordered the establishment of a International Military Tribunal and appointed Robert Jackson as chief prosecutor. Bernays gradually dropped out. And he played no role whatsoever in Nuremburg. He was this genius who invented the whole scheme and then had no impact whatsoever on the exit, as to how the scheme was put in place. But now at last gradually a division of roles between international courts and national or local courts is becoming visible.

Inflation of the Word 'Genocide'

Q: Genocide. Could we speak of inflation of the word genocide? Has it become the ultimate stamp of suffering? We see that victims who do not get that stamp feel let down, humiliated. The press writes that the prosecution failed, even if it proved other large-scale crimes against humanity.

C: Yes, genocide has become the 'magic word', as a US political scientist recently wrote. One reason is that people think that if massive crime is called genocide, the international community has a legal duty to do something about it. Totally wrong. There is no particular legal obligation incumbent on the international community to intervene in the case of genocide. In this respect there is, legally speaking, no difference whatsoever between crimes against humanity and genocide. In the case of genocide, you have a provision in the Genocide Convention whereby any member state can bring the question of genocide to the General Assembly or the Security Council, to the competent UN bodies. That's all. This is what every country can do in any case, even for natural catastrophes or for civil wars or for other mass violations of human rights. Therefore, arguing that a particular massacre amounts to genocide serves only a psychological and media purpose. Why? Because genocide is linked to the idea of the Holocaust. The quintessential genocide is the so-called Holocaust (a word I refuse to use because it means sacrifice. It was not a sacrifice; it was the massive killing of Jews). However, I would add, behind the psychological halo of this word, there is also one point of crucial importance. In the case of genocide, more than in any other crime against humanity, you have the atrocious attack on a whole group. Not so much on a whole community. Take the bombing of Dresden; that was the bombing of a community, but not a group united by a religion or ethnicity. Genocide underlines the discriminatory and persecutory nature of the destruction, the killing of people only because they belong to one religion, only because they are of Italian or Kurdish origin, for example.

The problem with genocide is not the definition. The definition is all right except for one thing, it's that the definition uses the word race – a notion that's proved wrong by anthropologists and so on. There's no race. Actually, you never say the Tutsis have been killed because of their race. The Jews have never made up a race. The concept of race was invented in the 19th century. Anthropologists and biologists now say that there are no races. There are groups with a common language, tradition, culture or religion, but there is no race.

The ICTR jurisprudence launched this idea of the subjective perception of genocide. This notion of the ICTR goes back to the case against Akayesu, the first genocide convict, and gradually they have developed this very important notion.

The distinction may not necessarily be a distinction based on objective features. Not between black and white skin color for instance. If both are black, both Catholic or Protestant, they may still belong to different groups. They *perceive* each other as members of two opposing groups, and this is what happened to the Hutus and Tutsis. Just as we see in Darfur with the so-called Arabs and Africans, where they have the same color, same language, same religion; they are both Muslims in Darfur. The Hutu and Tutsi are similar, they have the same religion and same color; they intermarried. The difference between the groups was a Belgian creation because the Belgians imposed the identity card in 1932. The Belgians were almost more horrible as colonizers than the Italians in Libya. They used the Tutsi against the Hutu, they needed the distinction in their power play.

In Darfur, from my viewpoint there's no distinction, either. However, I understand that gradually, because the so-called Arabs are despising the other groups, calling them slaves, the psychological, namely, subjective perception has led people of one group to think they belong to one group as opposed to another group.

In the Nuremburg judgments, we do not find the word genocide. We find, with regard to Jews, the word persecution, because in 1946 the word genocide was not yet deep-rooted in the international community. It was before the Genocide Convention. But still the Nuremburg Tribunal in its judgment was very powerful in saying that one of the worst crimes against humanity committed by the Nazis was persecution on reason of race, religion or political views.

There are several good, interesting judgments on genocide, in particular the *Krstic* judgment on Srebrenica at the ICTY. Patricia Wald, a fine American judge, drafted it. The Bosnian Serb General Krstic was Mladic's right hand when they took over the enclave Srebrenica. In the judgment you'll find an excellent exposition of the law, of why killing only the Muslim men, together with so many other elements, actually amounted to genocide. In the Darfur situation I do not think it is necessary to charge genocide. I hope that the ICC court of appeal will not follow the prosecutor, who wrongly claims that the fact that the women around the camps are being raped shows that they are destroying the group as such. But they don't do that because they want to destroy the group, but because they are horrible people who like to rape girls of 13. These are police officers, these are soldiers, Janjaweeds, simply going there for their pleasure, as sad and as simple as that, for their pleasure. Just to rape a girl of 13. This horrible misconduct amounts to a crime against humanity. Not however, to genocide, because what is lacking is the genocidal intent (the intention to attack somebody to destroy the whole group to which she or he belongs).

I asked many Sudanese men in camps of internally displaced persons (IDPs) when I was there, why they did send their female children to collect wood? They answered that it is not dignified for a man to fetch wood. I told them: if I had a daughter of 12, I would go with a lot of men, I would protect her, even if I did feel (which I do not!) it was not dignified for a man to collect wood.

Q: How do the men react when their daughters and wives are raped?

C: They kick them out. The girls and women are kicked out by the family. Therefore, they not only suffer from the horrible indignity of being raped but are also penalized, in a way, by their own family. Their plight is thus tremendous. On top of that, if they report to the police that they have been raped and are unable to identify the rapist, they may be prosecuted for adultery, which is a crime entailing the death penalty and can be committed either by a married woman or by an unmarried girl (in Sudan, adultery is any sexual intercourse with a person other than one's husband).

Q: If the women have become tainted by rape, and outcast as a result, can it not be said that the effect is to destroy the group?

C: No. The women as such do not constitute a 'protected group'. If they are attacked on a massive scale, for instance, they are raped, such massive rape can amount to a constitute element of genocide if you prove that the ethnic or religious or national or racial group to which the women belong is also being attacked. This is not the case here. Let me give you an example. When I was in the Kalma camp, there were 60,000 or so people. Now I think there are more than 100,000. It's a huge town made up of tents. If police officers or Janjaweed rape 20 or 30 or 50 girls from the camp who go out to collect wood, can you argue that such rapes are a means of destroying the group? In other words, do the rapes constitute the objective element of a subjective intention or *dolus specialis*, namely genocidal intent, or in other words the intent to destroy the whole group through the rapes? I would not say so. To me, those rapes amount to a terribly serious crime against humanity. Otherwise, can one justify the fact that the whole rest of the Internally Displaced Persons living in the same camp (100,000 persons, as I said) are not starving or dying because the Sudanese authorities allow international humanitarian organizations to provide food, water and shelter?

Q: Can you imagine, with hindsight, that the ICTY would have said what happened in Bosnia was not a genocide? At a conference, several notable jurists raised the question of whether genocide had not become more of a legal problem than a solution in international criminal law, since it had become so politicized and thus burdened the international courts with expectations that almost force the court to go for the severest charge, genocide.

C: I can tell you that some time ago in a discussion with other international lawyers, many argued that what happened in Srebrenica was not a genocide.

The *Krstic* judgment is very well argued, and probably if I had been there, I would have made a huge effort to say that it was genocide. But probably one could also argue that it only amounted to a whole range of crimes against humanity, namely persecution plus forcible expulsion plus extermination. Probably the Serbs did not want to destroy the whole Muslim group as such but only remove the group from its area. Of course, it would be politically unacceptable to say so.

Q: This kind of expulsion will only increase in the future, when groups will be fighting about water, resources, food — with the climate change and the scarcity of many resources, people will be chased away, deported, terrorized, killed. That will be ethnic cleansing maybe, but will it be genocide?

C: There was the idea shared at some point by Eichmann to deport all the Jews to Madagascar. If that had been implemented, it would have been deportation, expulsion, but not genocide. However, at one stage, he embraced the view that the Jews should be killed. When he went to Auschwitz, he said we should give priority to the killing of children because one day, they can go to Israel and again continue the race. This is typical genocide. Eichmann said it to Rudolf Höss, the commandant of Auschwitz who was later hanged in Poland. While he was waiting to be hanged, he wrote his memoir, called *Commandant at Auschwitz*, and he described how Eichmann visited Auschwitz twice. There are parts of the Wannsee conference transcript written by Eichmann and then the famous speech by Himmler at Poznan which are the only typical documents where you have the *mens rea*, the intent to genocide. There he said, I am talking of *Ausrottung* (extermination). I don't mean expulsion, Himmler said, but extermination, destruction.

A New Convention on Crimes against Humanity in the Making

Q: You are aware that a proposal for a crimes against humanity convention and protocol are in the making. The idea is to give clear definitions of the crimes against humanity and to give guidelines for national legislators, thus making the implementation of international criminal law and the Rome Statute and local prosecutions easier.

C: I think there's no point in drafting a new convention to define those crimes. There's a huge risk of losing much of what has been established. Customary international law is a very good basis. And then, the Rome Statute has added a couple of categories, which were useful apart from the crime of apartheid, which is a questionable addition, given that apartheid is a historical phenomenon that luckily is dead forever. They added forced pregnancy as a crime against humanity and other categories to protect women. That was good. However, it would be extremely useful to have a convention not on the definitions of the crimes against humanity, but only laying down procedural obligations, that is, providing for the duty of each contracting party to bring to trial people accused of crimes against humanity, to extradite them and to cooperate with each other and with the ICC.

Q: That could be a reason then for states not to sign the treaty on crimes against humanity?

C: But then there would be some sort of pressure on states. You know in Italy, we ratified the UN 1984 Torture Convention. However, because of the right wing, no law implementing the legislation has yet been passed, with the consequence that in Italy we don't have the crime of torture. Even after having ratified this Convention 10 years ago. It's really outrageous. There should be great pressure from the international community, so that the Conventions are finally implemented in my country.

Victims in International Criminal Courts

Q: The role of victims in the ICC has the makings of a quagmire. Some of your experienced colleagues now believe that the heavy accent on the role of victims at the ICC has not been such a good idea.

C: I know the problem. I think at the start, many people were enthusiastic about allowing victims to play a strong role, and it appears that the system has become hard to handle. Probably, it was wrong to allow the victims to participate in the proceedings at a very early stage. This could create a sort of bottleneck. My reaction would be to focus on what we've done here at the Special Tribunal for Lebanon. In light of the experience of the ICC and the huge problems emerging, we have decided first to exclude victims from the early phase, when charges are being confirmed. In domestic trials, say involving traffic accidents, the number of victims is small. At the international level normally one deals with collective crimes, in particular crimes against humanity, genocide or terrorism. These crimes involve thousands of victims. So, are you going to allow all of them to participate? What are the criteria? We decided early on to adopt a very narrow definition of victim: somebody who suffers direct damage from the crime. We decided to be strict and give the pre-trial judge the right to decide which victims should be allowed to participate in the proceedings. He may also decide that a group of, say, 30 people may be represented by only one lawyer. We need to avoid an imbalance, because you can immediately perceive that the victims are always on the side of the prosecution. We thought that would penalize the defense, which would have to fight not only against the prosecution but also against the lawyers of the victims. We will test the waters. If after two or three trials, the victims in court have proved too vocal, then we have another option, namely not to allow victims to call witnesses, but let only the trial chamber call such witnesses. Whatever they want to do, they have to go via the judges. We have professional judges, who will do this screening. This is how we hope to manage.

Also, unlike the ICC, the STL Statute rules out the role of *parties civiles*, the victims don't have a right to demand compensation.

Plea Agreements and Remorse
....

Q: Americans and other common law lawyers assign importance to plea-bargaining. Is there a place for this in war crimes courts? To lawyers, the benefits may be obvious, but to victims or spectators from countries not used to this, which is much of the world, it may appear that some people get off easy. It has been seen as a betrayal, a humiliation of the victims. War crimes trials or human rights trials are so different from domestic trials because of the scale of the wrongdoing.

C: I think there is a place for plea agreements. A suspect who decides to spill the beans can be of crucial importance. Often, these are conspiratorial crimes involving a group of people. So, an agreement with an insider may allow us to reach the heart of the crime. If I were a prosecutor, I would even be prepared not to prosecute, to grant immunity in exchange for compelling evidence. We would never have known how they managed to kill Giovanni Falcone, the Italian magistrate who was specialized in mafia crimes, if there had not been an agreement with a man who had himself committed horrible murders, but who was the only one available who could tell how it happened. He had been part of it. So, it may be the only way. When I went to Darfur with the Commission of Enquiry, on behalf of the Security Council, I asked Carla Del Ponte for advice. She said: you have to find an insider. If you don't, you are lost. She was right. We got very high up in the Sudanese system, to senior military, and they provided much information subject to the condition that their name would remain secret.

Q: But there have been plea agreements at the ICTY without the accused being helpful to the prosecution.

C: Mistakes have been made. But anyhow, it means prosecutors did not have to spend a lot of money on the case, and they had a guilty plea, setting out in detail whatever the accused participated in. The plea of former Rwandan prime minister Jean Kambanda was very important. He confessed to genocide, and in his plea, details of the massive crimes are listed.

Q: Is that enough truth?

C: It is not enough truth for the victims and for history.

Q: But for whom is this done then? The preferred and politically correct answer is: for the victims.

C: Not only for the victims. For international order. The international community must send a very clear message that we cannot condone such serious misconduct by a prime minister. A prime minister cannot be allowed to order the killing of almost one million of his nationals.

Q: By avoiding a trial, it does not fulfill its stated role, the role of healing, the truth-telling, establishing the record, all those goals people believe the international war crime tribunals should try to strive for. If we take short cuts for the sake of efficiency and cost saving, isn't there a contradiction?

C: The historical record is not of such crucial importance if you have other cases. And the victims should be satisfied that a perpetrator has been put in prison, maybe for 30 years or even for life. Victims may also cry, not for justice, but for revenge. The role of criminal justice should be to channel the quest for revenge by the victim, which should mitigate this thirst for revenge, which is a very primitive, archaic attitude of human beings. A key question is: what is the real interest of society compared with the interest of individuals crying for vengeance? On reflection, the major role of criminal justice is to reconcile the interest of individuals, particularly victims, with the public interest, but the public interest must always prevail.

Q: Did you ever see any real remorse in your career?

C: For a judge, it is very difficult to see remorse. I was in so many trials, but only once I saw remorse, in Drazen Erdemovic. He was a young man who admitted to having killed many Muslims in the Srebrenica area. He cried when he said, I had refused to take part in the killing, but the commander of the execution squad threatened me with death if I dropped out. So I had to accept under duress. I went on killing because I have a wife and a small child. Genuine remorse, I think, is very important. On that occasion I saw that somebody as human as I am happened to commit a crime because he found himself in the maelstrom of war. He was a young man, not very well educated. I had the fortune of being born when our war was about to be over and to have parents with some money to give me an education. I know that Erdemovic committed terrible crimes, he killed maybe 70 people, but I saw that he was really repenting, that this was genuine.

Q: Is the courtroom the best place to find a genuine expression of remorse? People play a role. They may start believing that they were right, that the prosecutor is the new enemy. If they show remorse, it could be a new façade.

C: I agree. It would be important if one could go to see a detainee and talk to him in private. Did you see this wonderful movie, *Judgment at Nuremberg*, with Spencer Tracy? I used to show it to my students regularly. At the end, Spencer Tracy as the presiding judge and the convicted minister of justice had a chance to speak. The judge respected this accused who had the guts to say: we were committing a crime; you are all cowards, all of you my co-defendants, for not admitting that. But then he tried to justify himself. And then the judge told him that at that very moment, he started breaching the principles of law and morals, he engaged in criminal conduct. I am mentioning it because this was a private conversation, and I think it would be very good if it was allowed for a judge to go and talk to an accused before sentencing. A two-hour talk between two human beings, off the record, about what he felt at that time. I would want to know whether somebody is genuine, and maybe thought twice about what he did.

To read body language may be misleading. Let me give an example. We had the case of Slavko Dokmanovic at the ICTY. Dokmanovic had been a mayor in Croatia who sided with the Serbs. He was terribly depressed, and I was so sorry because I too sometimes suffer depressions now and then. This poor man, I think he was not really guilty of the major crimes ascribed to him by the prosecution. The whole trial he looked so sad, depressed. I urged the prison guard to check with the medical doctor. Then at the end, he decided to testify, and all of a sudden he became a very lively man, and he testified very well on his own behalf. And then I told the other two judges that I didn't understand this man. He always looked so depressed, he never looked at me, and I was the presiding judge. Now he looks at me, he has a sort of dialogue with me, physical body language and so on, he smiles, he responds to my questions. I asked him a lot of questions. I was very inquisitive. I think too much because I was not a very good judge, so I was in a way overdoing it. Then, as soon as the trial was over, he hanged himself in jail, before we were able to issue our verdict. Afterwards it was explained to me that this was a phase. When you decide to kill yourself, then you feel free. You are no longer under your depression. You have made your decision. His body language was therefore a total deception. Not a willing deception, he didn't want to deceive me because he had decided in any case that he was going to kill himself. And we actually thought he was a very minor defendant, and we thought he didn't deserve any serious penalty. But he had decided to kill himself, and that's why the whole body language was completely misleading.

Q: You have a quotation of Bertolt Brecht on the wall of your office at the Lebanon Tribunal: '*Von Natur bin ich ein schwer beherrschbarer Mensch. Autorität, die nicht durch meinen Respekt entsteht, verwerfe ich mit Ärger, und Gesetze kann ich nur als vorläufige und fortwährend zu ändernde Vorschläge, das menschliche Zusammenleben regulierend, betrachten.*' (*I am by nature a man who is difficult to control. I reject with outrage any authority that does not rest on my respect. And I regard laws only as provisional and soon to be changed proposals for regulating human intercourse*) What is its meaning for you?

C: Well, I have always loved the plays and poems by Bertolt Brecht. I remember I went to visit his tomb in East Berlin in 1956 (I was a university student) one month after his death, and a few years later I visited the house where he had lived (which is now a museum) and again his tomb, in the small cemetery attached to his house, where you can find many other famous German poets and thinkers. That sentence that I have on my wall is self-explanatory, I assume; it expresses some skepticism about harsh laws, suggests that laws may and should be improved if they are not up to reality. It sets forth a strong opposition to any superior body not grounded in respect for human dignity.

¶

BENJAMIN FERENCZ

Removing the Lock from the Courthouse Door*

Reconciling Legitimate Concerns

BENJAMIN B. FERENCZ

The Problem

The International Military Tribunal (IMT) at Nuremberg held that aggression was 'the supreme international crime' for which leading planners and perpetrators could be held accountable in an international court of law. The legal recognition in 1946 that war-making was not a national right but an international crime was the greatest achievement of the trial and the proudest accomplishment of Robert M. Jackson, the highly esteemed US Supreme Court judge who served as Chief Prosecutor for the United States. Jackson made it clear that if law is to serve a useful purpose, 'it must condemn aggressions by any other nations, including those who sit here now in judgment'. The trial was 'part of the great effort to make the peace secure'. Subsequent Nuremberg proceedings and Tokyo war crimes tribunals confirmed the profound IMT decision.

The first General Assembly of the United Nations also affirmed the Nuremberg principles. Successive UN committees were appointed to draft an international criminal code to be enforced by a permanent international criminal court. Fifty-two years later, on 17 July 1998, a new International Criminal Court (ICC) was finally approved after a hectic five-week conference of plenipotentiaries that met in Rome. The acclaim for the ICC was overwhelming. The Rome Statute authorized the creation of a new international tribunal to bring leading perpetrators of genocide, crimes against humanity and major war crimes to justice. Aggression was included as one of the four 'core crimes', but the ICC was prohibited from exercising jurisdiction over that offense. Why not?

International law does not grow in a political vacuum. Some political leaders who hold the destiny of peoples in their power still do not see clearly enough the dire consequences of their failure to criminalize aggressive war. Ingrained traditions, symbols and slogans and outmoded notions of state sovereignty obscure the need for change. Article 5 (2) of the Rome Statute prohibited the ICC from trying anyone for the crime of aggression until, and unless, certain onerous conditions were fulfilled. Powerful states wanted the freedom to use their power, including the use of armed force to protect their perceived vital interests. Weak states wanted a firm legal shield to protect them from aggressors. There was insufficient time in Rome to hammer out an agreement on such a contentious issue that had vexed diplomats for decades. In a last minute compromise, the intransigent aggression problem was pushed to a back burner for later consideration. An Annex stipulated that amendments could be taken up at a Review Conference which could deal with the definition of aggression and "the conditions under which the International Criminal Court shall exercise its jurisdiction with regard to this crime". What that meant was:

1. aggression should be newly defined, and
2. agreement should be reached on the relationship between the ICC, which wanted to be independent, and the UN Security Council that wanted to control the show. Many expected or hoped that the crime of aggression would remain in limbo.

THE ADOPTED STATUTE contained clauses that some considered obstacles and others regarded as safeguards. Before the ICC would be enabled to try any aggressor, at least 60 nations would have to ratify the Statute (surprisingly, that minimum was surpassed as early as July 2002, thus putting the Statute into effect). Seven years would have to elapse before an amendment conference could be convened. The prescribed procedures for amendments were neither simple nor clear. A whopping seven-eighths of the Parties would have to agree to changes. Ratification would also be necessary, and those States that did not ratify would not be bound by the provisions on aggression (Art. 121). If the stalemate could not be broken, potential aggressors would certainly not be deterred but more likely encouraged to flaunt their immunity by continuing to defy the world community.

The Definition of Aggression

OPPONENTS OF THE court argued that aggression was not adequately defined and was thus subject to possible abuse by a politically motivated prosecutor. In fact, a 'consensus definition' was reached and approved by the General Assembly in 1974 after about 25 years of intense wrangling by successive special committees. The final definition, like most compromises, was laced with ambiguous clauses to enable parties to interpret it to suit their own political advantage. Permanent Members of the Security Council who were less than enthusiastic about an ICC inserted a clause that the definition was only advisory. Those opposed to an ICC also argued that the definition was intended only as a non-binding guide to the Security Council. The original assignment was linked to the Nuremberg precedents and made no reference whatsoever to the UN Security Council. Opponents of the ICC then argued that the definition did not conform to 'principles of legality' because it left the final determination to an unfettered decision of the Security Council. It was not noted that many valid criminal statutes contain vague phrases, such as 'fair trial', 'due process', and similar clauses that require judicial interpretation. The imprecision was caused by the same Security Council members who now complained that it was too imprecise.

The fact that the crime of aggression has already been adequately defined was asserted in 1945 by Justice Jackson and upheld in the judgments of the International Military Tribunal and confirmed by the General Assembly in 1946. It was endorsed, after comprehensive study, by the esteemed International Law Commission experts in 1996. Several renowned scholars, like Prof. Cherif Bassiouni and Prof. Claus Kress, and a host of other highly regarded authors maintain that aggression is a customary international crime that requires no further definition and is subject to universal jurisdiction as a peremptory norm from which there can be no derogation. The very distinguished British Law Lord Bingham of Cornhill hit the nail on the head when he stated in a 2006 case, '... the core elements of the crime of aggression have been understood, at least since 1945, with sufficient clarity to permit the lawful trial (and, on conviction, punishment) of those accused of this most serious crime. It is unhistorical to suppose that the elements of the crime were clear in 1945 but have since become in any way obscure' (House of Lords Judgments -R.v.Jones 92006 UKHL 16).

Every principle of legality has been protected by detailed rules of the ICC assuring fair trial to every defendant. It is unimaginable that any competent prosecutor would seek to indict anyone for the crime of aggression if the accused might reasonably argue that he couldn't really know that his deeds were criminal. The decoy argument that the defendant cannot get a fair trial because the crime of aggression has not been adequately defined is simply not persuasive. No new definition of aggression is needed.

The Relationship of the Court to the Security Council

A MORE DIFFICULT dilemma is posed by the fact that all parties seem agreed that the ICC should be independent yet it is unavoidably linked to the Security Council in the UN Charter as well as the Rome Statute. The International Law Commission has logically concluded that until an act of aggression has taken place, no individual can be held accountable for the crime. Who decides? The 1974 definition of aggression was absolutely clear that, in the last analysis, it was up to the Council to decide whether any act of a State was legally permissible or impermissible. The UN Charter, which binds everyone, charges the Council with the responsibility to determine whether an act of aggression by a State has taken place (Art. 39). Council decisions are influenced more by political than legal considerations. The Permanent Members have special veto rights, and this preference is understandably resented by those who do not share such a privilege. Fearing a biased Council, less privileged States would like to unlink the ICC from the Security Council. Consideration has therefore been given to by-passing the Council and turning to other bodies, such as the General Assembly or the International Court of Justice, to decide whether a State has acted unlawfully. Each alternative posed new problems.

In addition to UN Charter mandates, the Rome Statute itself imposes significant restraints on the independence of the ICC. The Security Council has the power to halt any ICC proceeding for an indefinite time (Art. 16). The Statute allows any State to divest the ICC of jurisdiction if it is willing and able to try the accused in its own national courts (Art. 17). Thus, if a country adopts the Rome Statute as part of its national criminal code, the ICC can be eliminated from the picture. Furthermore, if a State wishes to be immune from prosecution for aggression, all it has to do is fail to ratify whatever aggression amendment may be enacted (Art. 121). Numerous and complex procedural safeguards and pre-trial filters are additional impediments that may hamper prosecution. It should be recalled that investigations within the borders of hostile States and enforcement of sentences remain largely dependent upon the Security Council. The Security Council's involvement with the ICC and the crime of aggression is firm and unbreakable. The frustration of smaller States is fully understandable, but those who still insist upon the ICC's 'independence' should recognize that they are clinging to something they have already given away. They are unwittingly arguing about protecting the contents of an empty bag.

If the current efforts to bypass Security Council influence is abandoned by those who mistrust the Council, what can they expect in return? Once it is recognized that Security Council concerns are already adequately safeguarded by the UN Charter and the Rome Statute itself, it becomes clear that no more protection is needed. Nations that nevertheless insist on additional guarantees inevitably generate suspicion and hostility. On the other hand, foregoing new demands for more restraints on the ICC would earn appreciation and goodwill instead of fear and resentment by the state parties. The Security Council will be seen as a partner rather than an adversary of the ICC – which is as it should be. But logic can be trumped by political considerations that must also be taken into account. As long as the military may be required to intervene with armed force in situations which political leaders proclaim are purely defensive or a humanitarian intervention, commanding officers can hardly be expected to welcome the existence of any international court to test the legality of their military action. There can be no doubt that the best way to protect the lives of those who serve in the armed forces is to deter the crime of aggressive war. The Supreme Commander during World War II, Dwight Eisenhower, warned the nation after he became President of the United States that 'the world no longer has a choice between force and law. If civilization is to survive, it must choose the rule of law'. That conclusion was echoed by General Douglas MacArthur, commander of forces in the Pacific, as well as very many others who have experienced the indescribable horrors of warfare. Unfortunately, such views are not universally shared. It is therefore important to try to halt the glorification of war by condemning its atrocities as unacceptable acts of inhumanity that are subject to punishment under the rule of law. How then should one respond if powerful states stubbornly insist upon keeping the courthouse locked with the Council holding the key regarding the crime of aggression?

A Compromise Solution

IF, DESPITE ALL the persuasions mentioned above, some States will not acknowledge that the current terms of the Rome Statute provide all the protection they need against unfair prosecution for aggression, a fall-back compromise position can be considered as a last resort to overcome the impasse. Even if the lock on the courthouse cannot be removed, a way can still be found to open a crack in the sealed door. A clause can be added (in Article 16 or elsewhere) to the effect that no one can be convicted of [charged with] the crime of aggression unless the Security Council has first determined [acknowledged] that a State has committed the act of aggression, which is the subject of the complaint. That's just what the Permanent Members have been clamoring for, and it is the most hotly contested bone of contention. The bitter pill can be sweetened, if necessary, by adding such generally accepted mandates as 'in conformity with justice and the principles of international law' or references to the fact that any ICC judge of the same nationality as the accused would have to recuse himself and not be involved in the case. Such obligations are already included under Article 21 of the Statute. Even if the Council fails to act, and the aggression issue lies dormant on the Council shelf, potential aggressors will know that they may be held to account. The deterrent effect, no matter how modest, is an improvement over the present immunity. Surely, something is better than nothing.

Where the Debate Now Stands

MANY SCHOLARLY BOOKS and articles have been written by learned professors and others offering good suggestions on how to improve the ICC Statute. The more amendments that are offered for consideration at the Review Conference, the more difficult it will be to focus and reach agreement on 'the supreme crime' of aggression. The mandate of the Rome Annex was primarily related to the definition of the crime and the relationship between Court and Council. Only when those two issues have been resolved should consideration be given to other improvements. Much progress has been made by the Special Working Group in reformulating a revised definition of aggression. In 1974, the consensus definition was specifically approved as an integrated and indivisible package. Severing various select clauses from the consensus definition runs the risk of inviting protracted debate at the Review Conference. Why take chances when no change in the existing definition is really necessary?

Progress has also been made by the Working Group in articulating alternatives still being debated regarding the relationship between the ICC and the Security Council. The options range from requiring prior Council consent before the prosecutor can launch an investigation, or requiring authorization from either the Pre-trial Chamber, the General Assembly or the International Court of Justice. None of these alternatives has received general support in the discussions thus far. Any proposed amendment that can gain the required overwhelming acceptance of the Assembly would be a victory if it advances the desired goal of preventing war. The net effect of failure to reach agreement at a Review Conference, now scheduled for 2010, is to continue the dangerous impunity of aggressors and potential aggressors indefinitely – which is the inevitable consequence that ICC members hoped to avoid.

Even if the Security Council fails to live up to its responsibilities to condemn State acts of aggression, the ICC need not remain helpless. There has never been a war without atrocities. Persons suspected of aggression may also be charged with crimes against humanity and war crimes, as well as genocide, if applicable. Such trials do not require statutory amendments or advance permission from the Security Council, and they will surely attract widespread public attention. Life imprisonment is the maximum penalty for all ICC crimes, including aggression. The ICC Prosecutor, subject to the prescribed controls, could commence his investigation of aggression, and his mandated report to the Secretary-General of the UN could be made public. If the Security Council has been derelict in its duties, and the prosecution for aggression is allowed to lie dormant, the Council members would be subject to the public outrage that would follow. The new information revolution offers new opportunities to arouse public opinion in support of the rule of law. The 'shame factor' may be the most effective enforcement tool available to the ICC. The court of public opinion is a powerful tool that cannot be ignored or suppressed.

Recommendation and Conclusion

THE BEST WAY to carry out the mandate of the Rome Annex is to accept an amendment that simply deletes Paragraph (2) of Article 5. Nothing more is needed. The Commentary can explain that, after further detailed deliberation by the open-ended Working Group, the conclusion was reached by consensus that no further definitions or changes were necessary, and all rights of the Security Council under the UN Charter and the Rome Statute are fully respected. If the Permanent Members still insist on an added guarantee, a sentence can be added to the effect that no trial for the crime of aggression can be commenced without prior approval [acquiescence] by the Security Council. (The beginning of Article 62, 'Place of Trial', may be an appropriate spot.) As noted above, this compromise concession, which may sound outrageous to some, in fact concedes nothing that has not already been given away. What it gains is a slight opening to the ICC that might deter some future aggressors. Is it worth the bother?

Since time immemorial, human history has glorified war as a Divine right leading to conquest, treasure and glory. The most important accomplishment of the Nuremberg trials was the condemnation of illegal war-making as a supreme international crime. That great step forward in the evolution of international humanitarian law must not be discarded or allowed to wither. The creation of many new international courts, including the ICC, despite start-up shortcomings, demonstrates that international law is on the march for the betterment of people everywhere. Making it possible for the ICC to have jurisdiction over aggression, even if it seems remote today, would be a historical achievement of incalculable significance for a more peaceful world in the future.

Note
....

*   Published: May 2008. Source: Web Posting

Compensating Victims of the Crimes of War*

Benjamin B. Ferencz

WE ARE REMINDED by a distinguished former judge of the High Court of Calcutta that it is a timeless axiom of justice without which social life is unthinkable, that a wrong done to an individual must be redressed by the offender himself or by someone else against whom the sanction of the community may be directed.[1]

There can be no doubt that wrongs on a massive scale have been committed in Southeast Asia and that as a general rule large numbers of innocent persons have been the victims. As a result of the exigencies created by modern warfare, the United Nations has recently been exploring the measure of compensation which should be paid to victims of 'war crimes' and 'crimes against humanity'.[2] At present, some human rights conventions include provisions which call for compensation for such lesser violations as unlawful arrest and detention[3] or miscarriage of justice.[4] Under ordinary principles of tort law, those who engage in illegal or wrongful conduct must compensate the injured parties. Yet, as far as the victims of war crimes or crimes against humanity are concerned, 'the timeless axiom of justice' that the individuals who have been wronged are entitled to an appropriate form and measure of redress has largely been ignored.

Present practice permits considerable public attention to be attracted to all charges of violent crime and to the drama involved in the trial and punishment of the accused. But the needs of the victim are frequently ignored. Experience has shown that criminal sanctions, particularly if deemed inadequate, offer little solace and no assistance to the survivors. If justice is to be done, a more constructive alternative must be found. The payment of pecuniary damages by the offender is possible but not practicable. If the offender acted as the apparent agent of his government and with no malice of his own, it ought to be the duty of the State to redress the injury inflicted. It is suggested, therefore, that an organized program to compensate those who have been the victims of war crimes or crimes against humanity is worthy of serious consideration.

I   The Inadequacy of Penal Sanctions

EVER SINCE THE Nuremberg trials, it has been widely accepted as a principle of international law that the individual committing crimes against peace, war crimes, or crimes against humanity should be held criminally responsible, even if he acted under superior orders or was a head of state.

War crimes are generally held to be violations of the laws or customs of war. Such violations shall include but not be limited to murder, ill-treatment or deportation to slave labor or for any other purpose of the civilian population of or in occupied territory, murder or ill-treatment of prisoners of war or persons on the seas, killing of hostages, plunder of public or private property, wanton destruction of cities, towns or villages, or devastation not justified by military necessity.[5]

There was nothing novel about the prohibition of certain enumerated acts which had been declared unlawful in the Red Cross and Hague Conventions and which had been proscribed by the national law of most civilized states.

Although the underlying concept was old, the title of 'crimes against humanity' was something new, for 'Laws of Humanity' and 'dictates of the public conscience' had long been the subject of international consideration. Acts which ordinarily would have been considered war crimes acquired a new characterization if they were inhumane acts committed against a civilian population for political, racial or religious reasons and if they constituted large and systematic actions which were cloaked with official authority. By their dimension and brutality the collective conscience of mankind was shocked and such acts became international offenses which were now codified under a new caption.[6] Thus, the Nuremberg proceedings set down the three categories and the broad headings under which an individual might be prosecuted – at least in legal theory – for offenses committed in Southeast Asia.

Viewed realistically, these penal principles so firmly enunciated at Nuremberg and ratified in the halls of the United Nations have had very limited application since. It has become almost the anticipated allegation made by combatants that only their opponents are guilty of aggression and crimes against humanity. Not surprisingly, no one has been charged in a court of law with the commission of such offenses since 1945.

It is the unfortunate, if not absurd, truth that for nearly half a century, nations have been unable to agree on what they mean by aggression[7], and even if it could be defined, no court exists to try 'the gravest of all crimes throughout the world'.[8] It is the latest consensus view of the Special United Nations Committee to Define Aggression that only the Security Council should have authority to decide who is the aggressor. In a political arena with veto powers, a judicial determination is, under the present circumstances, hardly to be expected. It appears most unlikely in the foreseeable future that States will voluntarily accept the jurisdiction of any international court over problems affecting major national interests.[9] Moreover, the United States Supreme Court, as presently constituted, will not even listen to arguments that the United States is embarked on a war of aggression, since the conduct of foreign affairs is viewed as a non-justiciable Presidential or Congressional prerogative.[10]

As far as war crimes are concerned, the situation is a little, but not much, better. In 1955, the Supreme Court held that those who had left the military service could not be charged with crimes committed while in uniform.[11] Under the Geneva Conventions of 1949, our government was legally obliged to enact legislation to bring to trial all persons who had committed 'grave breaches' of the Convention, including willful killing or inhuman treatment of prisoners of war and civilians and the wanton destruction of property not justified by military necessity. Yet for over 17 years, no step was taken to close the ex-serviceman's escape hatch to immunity.[12]

In the face of such publicly disclosed tragedies as the My Lai massacre, a certain number of trials by court-martial against those soldiers or officers directly responsible for shooting helpless and innocent civilians was unavoidable. The military accusing one of its own of dereliction is surely a painful process. When the offense may have been stimulated by the Army's own failure to stress adequately humanitarian considerations, it is particularly embarrassing. Where the crimes are committed during a counter-insurgency action in which non-combatants and the enemy are often indistinguishable, the dilemmas facing the combat soldier evoke the sympathy not only of large segments of the public but also of the Commander-in-Chief. A comprehensive program of war crimes trials by an impartial court or by victors over the vanquished is obviously not on the horizon.

The mere fact that some war crimes trials were conducted by the United States against American soldiers during a period of 'war' is a rare phenomenon in a world which periodically seethes with armed conflict. However, the manner in which the trials were conducted, as well as their outcome, demonstrates that the military may not be relied upon to accuse and try itself.[13] Only a dozen men were ever charged with responsibility for the My Lai massacre, and all save one, Lt. William Calley, were found to have done no wrong.

Surely, no one will pretend that no other war crimes have been committed in Southeast Asia. Yet apparently no further criminal trials are contemplated. We have forgotten what was learned at Leipzig after World War I when the Germans in trying their own war criminals produced only six convictions out of 896 accused.[14] We have forgotten that after World War II we espoused the theory that the principles of international penal law apply to foe and friend alike. In the final analysis, we are reminded of the last words of Justice Robert H. Jackson as he closed the Nuremberg prosecution in the name of the United States:

> If you were to say of these men that they are not guilty, it would be as true to say there has been no war, there are no slain, there has been no crime.[15]

The military conviction of a single officer in a single case can only dramatize how ineffective has been the attempt to impart a feeling of vindication or justice through the conduct of military trials. In the absence of any effective criminal sanctions, it is all the more important that a meaningful civil remedy be sought. Let us examine the rights of the victims as we consider the obligations of the perpetrators of the crimes.

II   Civil Responsibility for Compensation

A   Responsibility of the Individual Offender

WHERE A SOLDIER has been convicted by a military court of having committed war crimes and that conviction is no longer subject to review, he will have been found guilty beyond a reasonable doubt of having deliberately committed the wrongful acts. The conviction will have established that his deeds were not acts of legitimate military necessity but were in fact illegal and contrary to the established rules of war. Under ordinary principles of civil law, he should be obliged to make compensation for property losses, personal injuries and loss of life.

The case would be the same if a superior officer were found to have failed negligently to exercise sufficient control over his troops to have prevented the occurrence of the offense,[16] or to have been negligent in the indoctrination and training of troops which were placed in a position where the commission of crimes reasonably could have been foreseen. It is the business and function of commanding officers to maintain a level of discipline and control over their armed forces adequate to restrain the power, the propensity, and the opportunity to commit unlawful acts. If the superior's neglect gave rise to the injury, there would be no substantial distinction between his negligence and the deliberate commission of the wrongful act in imposing civil liability for damages.

The matter would be more difficult where there was no prior conviction by a military court, for in those cases the plaintiff would have to prove in the civil action that the defendant was personally responsible for the commission of the illegal act. For the victim to obtain such evidence would almost certainly prove impossible. The unfortunate victims are often too terrorized, too uninformed or too powerless to even consider requesting the reparations to which they would be both legally and morally entitled.

Even if the facts of unlawful or negligent conduct could be established, the plaintiff would still face a host of problems. He would have to obtain jurisdiction over the defendant,[17] set forth specifically the alleged wrongful conduct, prove the extent of damages,[18] and be able to collect on whatever judgment might be issued. There would surely be a public outcry against holding a solider financially responsible for action taken in the belief, however badly mistaken, that he was serving his country. This public sentiment would be reinforced by the feeling that he had already paid his debt if there had been a conviction and sentence. It could be anticipated that in most cases of war crimes, the offender would be financially unable to satisfy the judgments rendered against him to compensate the victims.[19] Most often, the injured party would be left between the difficult predicament either of not being able to prove his case or of not being able to collect his award.

An action for $ 400 million brought against Lt. Calley, Secretary of Defense Laird, and Secretary of the Army Resor on behalf of the Unified Buddhist Congregation of Vietnam, purporting to represent the My Lai massacre survivors, was promptly dismissed by the United States District Court in Georgia. The decision was based on the plaintiff's lack of capacity to sue, failure to state a complaint and expiration of the two-year statute of limitations.[20] If justice is not to be defeated by the denial of real redress to the wronged individual who has a justified claim, an alternate basis of liability must be sought.

B   Responsibility of the State for Acts of Its Officers

THE RESPONSIBILITY OF States for damages caused to aliens has been the subject of intensive study by the International Law Commission[21] and was dealt with extensively in a draft convention prepared at Harvard University under the direction of Professors Sohn and Baxter.[22] There is a long tradition in the US of insisting, as a matter of law as well as equity, that a State is responsible for the acts of its officer done within the apparent scope of its authority.[23]

The theories under which the State is held responsible have varied.[24] In some cases the officer is viewed as the agent of his government, and liability attaches under ordinary principles of agency law. In other cases, liability is based on the State's negligence in either failing to prevent the offense or on a denial of justice by failing to find, try, and adequately punish the parties directly culpable. The dereliction is viewed as an omission for which the State is itself responsible. Therefore, the State would be deemed to have transgressed a provision of international law as the State's duties, and the government's negligence in not punishing the criminal has denied the offended party the opportunity of subjecting the wrongdoer to a civil suit.

The Geneva Conventions of 1949 require the US to enact any legislation necessary to provide effective penal sanctions against persons committing any grave breaches of the Convention, and to bring such persons, regardless of their nationality, before its own courts or to hand them over to trial by another High Contracting Party. It has been pointed out by Alfred P. Rubin that we have failed to live up to this international penal obligation.[25] If we also fail to live up to our civil obligations to indemnify the victim, we should not be surprised if our government is viewed as having condoned the offense or as having exercised actual or tacit complicity in the crimes.

The Hague Convention IV of 1907 provided that a belligerent who violated the regulations would be liable to make compensation. Article 3 prescribed responsibility 'for all acts committed by persons forming part of its armed forces'.[26] The US has regularly confirmed the principles of State liability and demanded compensation from foreign governments for wrongs committed by their officers against US nationals.[27] The US has also paid compensation when the wrongdoer was an officer of the US. A particularly apposite case involved a 2nd lieutenant Gulley, an American officer who in 1919 was on guard at the Mexican border. He shot at a raft in the Rio

Grande, intending only to frighten the occupants whom he believed to be engaged in illegal activities. One of the shots killed a Mexican girl. The action of the lieutenant was an error of judgment for which he was convicted by court-martial and discharged. He was restored to duty by the President of the US. The Mexican-American Claims Commission required the US to pay compensation to the parents of the slain girl.[28] If the US had to pay for the unintentional killing by Lt. Gulley, should it not also be responsible for the intentional killing by Lt. Calley?

Many years ago M. Henry Frimageot, the distinguished French member of the Permanent Court of International Justice, enunciated the general rule that a Government is responsible for errors in judgment of its officials purporting to act within the scope of their duties.[29] No one has claimed that Lt. Calley, or his like, as callous as may have been their deeds, were acting with a malice of their own. American servicemen, who may have committed war crimes, whether recklessly, carelessly, or in direct contravention of their orders, were nevertheless purporting to act within the scope of their duties as soldiers. It is the legal and moral obligation of the government in whose name and on whose behalf the deeds were committed to see to it that the victims of the crimes receive just compensation for the injuries unlawfully inflicted upon them.

III   A Suggested Program of Constructive Action

THE EXTENT OF US involvement in 'war crimes' or 'crimes against humanity' is a hotly debated subject, often influenced by the participants' emotional reaction to the war itself. Although it is certain that war crimes have also been committed by the other combatants, it is only the US which has sought to restrain such illegal deeds by the trial and public condemnation of at least a few of the offenders. The US government should, therefore, continue to assert its moral leadership by not making its adherence to international law and precedent dependent or conditional on the similar action by any other State.

A   Defining the Perimeter of Criminal or Civil Liability

THERE HAS BEEN considerable debate and disagreement about what actions in Southeast Asia might be considered sufficiently criminal to give rise to an obligation to indemnify the civilian victims. The range of possible offenses covers a wide spectrum. At one end there are such clear war crimes as the deliberate killing of helpless civilians at My Lai and similar atrocities. Here both the criminal and the civil liabilities are beyond dispute. At the other extreme, however, are such difficult questions as the legality of the war itself, and whether the interventions in North Vietnam, Laos and Cambodia were aggressive acts constituting 'crimes against peace' or whether they were lawful acts of legitimate self-defense and retaliation. In the absence of all of the records on all sides, it is not likely that these questions will be authoritatively resolved in the near future. It is more productive therefore to deal with the areas where some agreement may be possible.

The problems which have evoked the most heated public debate among qualified observers are related to the legality of 'free-fire zones', 'search and destroy' operations, destruction of undefended areas by artillery or bombing, the use of chemical defoliants, the resettlement of villages, and the detention of civilians as well as the methods of interrogating prisoners.[30] The UN has long been concerned with increasing respect for human rights during periods of armed conflict.[31] The International Committee of the Red Cross has convened an inter-governmental conference to improve the rules of warfare in an attempt to make them more reflective of the needs of our times.[32] But since States continue to be concerned primarily with protecting their own legal and political positions, it is not likely that there will be any early clarification that will end the debate about the legality of various actions in Vietnam.

The Bar Association of the City of New York, assisted by a panel of very distinguished American jurists, recently proposed that a commission, including leaders of the Bar, the Congress, the public and the armed forces, be appointed to investigate and report on the observance of the laws of war in Indochina.[33] Particular attention would be paid to the type of problems indicated above. If our government would agree to the establishment of such a commission, it could also have as one of its responsibilities the obligation to set forth those areas in which the United States would be willing to assume financial responsibility for war-related damages. This could be done without necessarily acknowledging any criminal responsibility for violating any of the present laws of war. The commission could define the parameters within which the US would be prepared to make compensation on either legal or humanitarian grounds.

B   Legislation for Individual Compensation

ONCE THE PRINCIPLES of liability have been accepted, it will be necessary to draw up the precise statute or rules and regulations which will govern the payment of compensation. These would set forth the classes of persons eligible for payment, the categories of damage for which compensation would be paid (personal, property or economic losses), the elements of proof required after taking into account what may reasonably be demanded, the measure of compensation for the different types of loss, and the procedure for disposing of the claims as well as for the review of decisions reached.

What can be done to help is not as difficult as it may seem. History has never recorded crimes of the magnitude committed by the Hitler regime of Nazi Germany.[34] Yet after World War II, an enormous program was instituted for providing restitution and indemnification to surviving victims of that holocaust.[35] In addition to the return of hundreds of thousands of properties and businesses,[36] the Federal Republic of Germany provided individual compensation to over three million victims of persecution. Over $ 10 billion have been paid in indemnities for loss of life, loss of profession, false imprisonment, permanent damage to health and various economic deprivations.[37] The payment of compensation to millions of victims of that war was accomplished without any noticeable hardship to the average German citizen. The wise German leaders, such as Chancellor Konrad Adenauer, considered restitution to Nazi victims to be an essential moral prerequisite for Germany's readmission to the family of civilized nations. The US assisted, encouraged and applauded the German action. Is it not time for the US to begin to follow its example?

C   The Administrative Machinery to Settle the Claims

WHERE CLAIMS ARE asserted against the government itself, it would be preferable to have the adjudication done by some impartial body. A neutral international court, such as the International Court of Justice, would be the ideal body to supervise the disposition of the claims. To comply with the Statute of the Court,[38] the case for the claimant could, as is customary in international law, be presented by his own government acting on his behalf. It would enhance the image of international law if the US would accept the jurisdiction of the under-utilized[39] World Court in the matter.

If the US remains reluctant to surrender its sovereignty to the Court in connection with war claims, perhaps it might consider allowing the International Committee of the Red Cross to deal with such claims on humanitarian grounds. This is what was done by the Federal Republic of Germany in connection with the claims of Nazi medical experiment subjects who resided in countries with which Germany had no diplomatic relations and which were, therefore, denied compensation under the general German indemnification laws.[40] The German action was largely in response to American public pressure.[41]

Resort can always be had to Mixed Claims Commissions, which have frequently been employed to settle claims of foreign nationals. Presumably, these would be composed of all, or at least some, of the States parties to the conflict, and claims could be adjudicated by nationals of all participants or neutral States. Such Commissions and arbitral tribunals have worked effectively in the past without any major problems.[42] There is also the precedent of the Philippine War Damage Commission, concerned primarily with rehabilitation,[43] and of the existing Foreign Claims Settlement Commission of the US, which adjudicates claims of American nationals for various types of war losses.[44] Probably the easiest way to handle the claims would be accomplished through bilateral agreements with the other States involved. The US would pay a fixed sum of money which the receiving State would then distribute among its nationals pursuant to agreed criteria and possibly under the supervision or control of the US.[45] Payment would be either by a lump sum or in installments. A wide variety of precedents and patterns are available. The administrative machinery to do the job can readily be created. All that is needed is the will to act.

D Reparations to Supplement Individual Indemnification

COMPENSATION ON THE basis of individual claims may be replaced or preferably supplemented by other forms of reparation. In many cases it may be impossible to identify the individual victims of conduct which the US is prepared to indemnify.[46] Where whole areas have been defoliated or destroyed, where the ecology of a region has been seriously disrupted, or where all the inhabitants of villages have been dislocated by flight or relocation, it may be possible to provide funds to help rebuild or replace what was destroyed. The construction of hospitals, homes, schools, orphanages, or the provision of food, supplies, or technical assistance may all be suitable forms of reparation. The local government can undertake the reconstruction or distribution subject to sufficient controls to assure that the objectives of the rehabilitation are achieved. President Nixon recently indicated that the US would be prepared to consider substantial grants to the countries in Southeast Asia as part of a reconstruction program.[47] His proposal was consistent not only with the traditional post-war reconstruction practice of the

US but also with our apparent legal obligations. Whatever else, it tended to re-emphasize the feasibility of the concept of compensating the victims of armed conflicts as proposed in this article.

IV Conclusion

PROFESSOR HYDE ONCE wrote: Control breeds responsibility. A State must be deemed to be internationally responsible for the consequences of internationally illegal conduct within any area over which it in fact asserts control in time of peace or war.[48]

The US should acknowledge its responsibility for wrongful conduct of its officers and start to plan and prepare the measures which will be required to compensate the victims of war crimes in Southeast Asia. Voluntary committees of Americans have already begun to take humanitarian action to aid the war-injured Vietnamese children and others.[49] Where our government cannot accept legal responsibility, it should act on the basis of humanitarian commitment. The American government has an opportunity and an obligation, which will help bind up the wounds both here and abroad. It should begin to act now.

Notes

* Published: April 1972. Source: *The Virginia Journal of International Law*, Volume 12, Number 3, April 1972.

The editorial assistance of Martin F. Conniff, a student at the University of Virginia School of Law, is gratefully acknowledged.

1 Roy, Is The Law of Responsibility of States for Injuries to Aliens a Part of Universal International Law?, 55 *Am.J.Int'l L.* 863 (1961).

2 G.A. Res. 2712, 25 U.N. GAOR Supp. 28, at 79, U.N. Doc. A/8233 (1970).

3 International Covenant on Civil and Political Rights, art. 9, 21 U.N. GAOR Supp. 16, at 58, U.N. Doc. A/6546 (1966); European Convention on Human Rights and Fundamental Freedoms, art. 5, Council of Europe 3-4 (1971).

4 American Convention on Human Rights, art. 10.

5 Control Council Law No. 10, art. II, para 1(b), which set forth the principles under which the Nuremberg Military Tribunals were conducted.

6 See Ferencz, War Crimes, Law and the Vietnam War, 17 *Am.U.L.Rev.* 403 (1968); U.S. Dep't of State, Pub, No. 3080, Conference on Military Trials 395 (1945). See

also Dautricourt, La Définition du Crime Contra l'Humanite, [1947] *Revue de Droit Penal*. Professor Frank C. Newman: acts committed against a civilian population are crimes against humanity (unpublished paper submitted to a panel of the American Society of International Law, June 1971). He concludes that the United States may be committing crimes against humanity in Indochina.

7   Report of the Special Committee on the Question of Defining Aggression, 26 U.N. GAOR Supp. 19, at 21, U.N. Doc. A/8419 (1971).

8   See G.A. Res. 380, 5 U.N. GAOR Supp. 20, at 13, U.N. Doc. A/1775 (1950).

9   See Toward a Feasible International Criminal Court, chap. 26 (J. Stone & R. K. Woetzel eds. 1970); Falk, Realistic Horizons for International Adjudication, 11 *Va. J. Int'l. L.* 314 (1971).

10 Orlando v. Laird, 40 U.S.L.W. 3158 (U.S. Oct. 12, 1971); United States v. Mitchell, 246 F. Supp. 874 (D.C. Conn. 1965); see also Brief for the Constitutional Lawyers' Committee on Undeclared War, reprinted in 17 Vietnam, 57 Calif. L. REV. 1055 (1969).

11 Toth v. Quarles, 350 U.S. 11 (1955).

12 Rubin, Legal Aspects of the My Lai Incident, 49 *Ore.L.Rev.* 260 (1970). With respect to the protection of civilian persons, see Geneva Conventions, Aug. 12, 1949, art. 147, [1956]. T.I.A.S. No. 3364.

13 See Taylor, The Course of Military Justice, *N.Y. Times*, Feb. 2, 1972, at 37, col. 1.

14 S. Glueck, War Criminals , Their Prosecution and Punishment 311 (1944).

15 Nazi Conspiracy and Aggression 44 (Supp. A, 1947) (emphasis added).

16 See In re Yamashita, 327 U.S. 1 (1946); compare the case against Capt. Ernest L. Medina, the company commander of the convicted Lt. William Calley, which seemed to require actual knowledge that war crimes were being committed. Medina was acquitted. See *N.Y. Times*, Sept 26, 1971, §E, at 6; see also T. Taylor, Nuremberg and Vietnam: An American Tragedy (1970).

17 The federal district courts should have jurisdiction to deal with violations of treaties to which the US is a party, including treaties establishing the rules of war. 28 USC § 1350 (1970) provides: The District Courts shall have original jurisdiction of any civil action by an alien for a tort only, committed in violation of the law of nations or a treaty of the United States. The presence of the defendant in the armed forces should not serve as an insurmountable barrier any more than it would if the defendant could also be held accountable in the jurisdiction of his domicile. The domicile of the plaintiff could also serve as the forum if he could obtain jurisdiction over the defendant by personal service. There would seem to be a persuasive reason why the plaintiff could not assign his claim to someone domiciled elsewhere.

18 Damages would generally be determined by the financial loss sustained by those

dependant upon the victim and by the victim himself if he survived. It would not be unreasonable in the case of war crimes to demand and to expect punitive damages as well for their additional deterrent effect. A few States have denied punitive damages in the case of torts which are also crimes, and some have held that a conviction and fine in a criminal prosecution could be shown in mitigation of damages, but the great weight of authority would allow punitive damages where the defendant was guilty of willful disregard of the rights of others.

19 In the case of some convicted German war criminals who were enormously wealthy industrialists, such as Alfred Krupp, or multimillionaire concerns such as I.G. Farben, AEG, Telefunken, and others, it was possible to obtain compensation for survivors of concentration camps. This was done, however, by way of negotiated settlements since the German courts refused, for purely procedural reasons, to deal with the substance of the claims. See Ferencz, West Germany: Supreme Court Bars Claims of Forced Laborers Against German Industrial Concerns, 15 *Am. J. Comp. L.* 561 (1967).

20 Civil Action No. 1473 (M.D.Ga. 1971). The case was dismissed on July 8, 1971.

21 See Amador, (First) Report on State Responsibility, [1957] 2 *Y.B. Int'l L. Comm'n* 173, U.N. Doc. A/CN. 4/96 (1956).

22 Harvard Law School, Convention on Injury to Aliens (1960); see also Harvard Draft on the Responsibility of States for Damages Caused on Their Territories to Persons and Property of Foreigners, 23 *Am. J. Int'l. L.* 131 (Special Number 1929).

23 As early as 1873, U.S. Secretary of State Fish defined a rule of the law of nations to the effect that a government which refuses to repair the damage committed (to aliens) by its citizens or subjects, to punish the guilty parties or to give them up for that purpose may be regarded as virtually a participant in the injury and as responsible therefore. J. B. Moore, 6 International Law Digest 655 (1906). In 1885 Secretary of State Bayard declared that the mere fact that an act might be committed without orders from superiors in command was not dispositive of the question of liability. He acknowledged that the US was responsible even if the soldiers' acts were forbidden, provided they were not motivated by private malice. J.B. Moore, 6 International Law Digest 758 (1906).

24 Professor Richard B. Lillich has edited the Procedural Aspects of International Law Series which deals with various aspects of international claims; see e.g., R. Lillich & G. Christenson, International Claims: Postwar British Practice (1967).

25 See note 12 supra; see also Brierly, The Theory of Implied State Complicity in International Crimes, 9 *Brit. Y.B. Int'l. L.* 42 (1928).

26 Hague Convention IV of 1907, art. 3, 36 Stat. 2277 (1909-11), T.S. No. 539.

27 A mixed claims commission set up under the Treaty of Berlin between the US and Germany, 3 U.S.T. 2596 (1921), dealt with claims arising out of the sinking of the

British liner Lusitania which was torpedoed by a German submarine with the loss of 128 American lives while the obligation to pay the US for the death, personal injury and property losses of the American nationals. It set forth an elaborate formula for determining the extent of compensation, taking into account such factors as the amount which the decedent, had he not been killed, would probably have contributed to the claimant, plus an amount for the loss of personal services, for pain and suffering and other elements similar to those usually applied in assessing damages in an ordinary negligence action. Lusitania Cases (US v. Germany), Mixed Claims Commission 1923; Cons. Ed. of Decisions 17 (1925). Our government also demanded and received compensation for injuries to American nationals by foreign soldiers from Canada, Honduras, Spain, Poland, Mexico, Venezuela, Israel, and many other countries.

28 Garcia and Garza v. US, General Claims Commission (1926), reprinted in 21 AM. J. INT'L. L. 581 (1927). The Associated Press reported on Aug. 1, 1971, that the US was paying $ 17 million to Vietnamese civilians for personal injury or property losses sustained when a US ammunition dump accidentally exploded. The Congressional Resolution No. 617 authorizing $ 25 million for World War II damage claims to inhabitants of US Trust Territories. CONG. Q., July 25, 1971, at 1371.

29 Quoted in H. Briggs, The Law of Nations 584 (1942). Many States provide benefits to the victims of ordinary crimes, and federal legislation has been introduced to compensate those who have been victims of domestic murders, rapes, and robberies. See *NY Times*, Dec. 12, 1971, at 95, col. 5; Lamborn, Remedies for the Victims of Crime, 43 S. CAL. L. REV. 22 (1970). Why should the US Government's obligation be less if the crime is committed by a soldier acting for the US?

30 See Sheehan, *NY Times*, Mar. 28, 1971, (Book Review), at 1, col. 1. In this piece Neil Sheehan reviews 33 books on the subject as submitted by Professor Mark Sachanoff.

31 U.N. Doc. A/8052 (1970); U.N. Doc A/8313 (1971).

32 See Carnegie Endowment, Report on Contemporary Problems of the Law of Armed Conflicts (1971); Hewitt, Recent Developments: Respect for Human Rights in Armed Conflicts, 4 N.Y.U.J. INT'L. L. & P. 41 (1971).

33 27 Record of the Association of the Bar of the City of New York (Jan. 1972).

34 See Nazi Conspiracy and Aggression (1946); Trials of War Criminals Before the Nuremberg Military Tribunals (1949).

35 See *Bundes Entschadigungsgetz* (Blessin-Ehrig-Wilden 1960); *Bundes Ruckerstattungsgegetz* (Blessin-Wilden 1958); *Bundes Entschadigungs-schlussgesetz* (Blessin-Gleisster 1967).

36 Restitution was effected pursuant to restitution laws of the three Western occupying powers. See U.S. Mil. Gov't Law No. 59 (Nov. 20, 1947); Mil. Gov't Law

59 of the U.K. of (May 12, 1949); Ordinance No. 120 of the French Commander (Nov. 10, 1947). See Ferencz, Restitution to Nazi VictimsA Milestone in Morality, Two Generations in Perspective (H. Schneiderman ed. 1957).

37   Official Statistics of the Federal Republic of Germany, Ministry of Finance; see also U.N. Doc. E.CN. 4/1010, at 23-26 (1969), for information concerning the criteria for determining compensation to the victims of war and crimes against humanity as set forth by many States.

38   See I.C.J. STAT. Art. 34, which provides that only States may be parties in cases before the Court.

39   See U.N. Doc. A/8405 (1971); see generally 11 VA. J. INT'L L. 291-371 (1971).

40   Decision of the Cabinet of the Federal Republic of Germany, July 16, 1951. See *Bundes Entschadigungsschlussgesetz* (Blessin-Giesler 1967), at 216, 306, 308, 839.

41   See Cousins, Report on the Ladies, *Sat.Rev.*, July 22, 1961, at 28.

42   See Agreement Signed at Berlin, Aug. 10, 1922, 3 U.S. treaties 2601; see also the work of the Mexican Claims Commission, reported in J. Moore, 2 Arbitration 1249-86 (1898), and the decisions of the Court of Restitution Appeals.

43   See Schein, War Damage Compensation Through Rehabilitation, The Philippine War Damage Commission, 16 *Law & Contemp. Prob.* 519 (1951).

44   See War Claims Act of 1948, 50 U.S.C. App. § 2017; Decisions of the Foreign Claims Settlement commission (U.S. Gov't Printing Office).

45   In the agreement between the State of Israel and the Federal Republic of Germany of Sept. 10, 1952, Israel undertook to compensate some of its own nationals for damage to their health caused by Nazi persecution. Germany paid reparation in the form of goods shipped over a ten-year period. 162 U.N.T.S. 206 (1953).

46   Apparently, no effort was made following the My Lai massacre to identify the victims who appeared in photographs to have been treated no better than cord wood. The US military should consider issuing regulations requiring that every effort be made to ascertain the next of kin of any civilians killed in areas controlled by the US. It would indicate humanitarian concern and an interest in possibly helping the survivors.

47   *N.Y. Times*, Jan. 26, 1972, at 10, col. 1. President Nixon's position was reiterated by Secretary of State Rogers, N.Y. Times, Feb. 7, 1972, at 12, col. 3.

48   C. Hyde, 2 International Law 922 (1945).

49   See the work of the Committee of Responsibility of War Injured Children, Washington, D.C.; see also an article in the *International Herald Tribune*, June 23, 1971, reporting on 200 scientists at a dozen American universities doing research to help 'the victims of US aggression in Vietnam'.

Seeking Redress for Hitler's Victims (1948-1956)[*]

Benjamin B. Ferencz

To avoid revenge and retaliation, victims of oppression must know that their oppressors have been brought to justice; and efforts must be made to heal the wounds of those who have suffered. There were no precedents for adequately coping with the Holocaust. New legal concepts and new laws were required. Restitution of expropriated property was only a beginning. Injuries had to be compensated, and new organizations were needed to help victims prove their claims. The programs of restitution, compensation, and legal assistance were all intertwined. Starting in 1948, I was deeply involved in all of these endeavors. Concentration camp victims who had survived with only their tattoos and scarred memories needed help urgently and desperately. The complexity of problems, and their solutions, could hardly be imagined.

Restitution of Confiscated Property

My administrative work in wrapping up the Office of the Chief of Counsel for War Crimes was almost over when my wife and I prepared to return home to a normal life. But I was unexpectedly recruited for a new assignment by a representative of the world's leading Jewish organizations. Military Government law provided that properties seized by the Nazis in the US zone of occupation should be returned to the rightful owners. If no owners or heirs could be found, the assets could be claimed by a charitable organization pledging to use the proceeds to benefit survivors of persecution. A consortium of prominent Jewish organizations formed the 'Jewish Restitution Successor Organization' (JRSO), and they needed someone to set up and manage such a challenging endeavor. They didn't really think anything much would come of it, and they were not prepared to invest their limited charitable funds into such an uncertain enterprise. Nevertheless, they felt it was their moral duty to try.

Their representative, an American lawyer named Joel Fischer, came to Nuremberg from the office of the American Jewish Joint Distribution Committee, a respected philanthropic organization, then headquartered in Paris. He said they wanted a two-year commitment. My wife, Gertrude, had never felt comfortable in Germany. Yet, the moral imperative of possibly being able to help Holocaust survivors (including some of her own relatives) could not be turned down. In August 1948, I accepted the job and designated myself the Director-General of the JRSO, knowing that Germans would be impressed by someone who was both a Director and a General. We did not imagine that ten years would pass from the time we left home before we could return to America – together with our four children, all born in Nuremberg.

The Military Government law under which the JRSO was to operate stipulated that all claims had to be filed by the end of 1948, only four months away. It seemed impossible to meet that deadline, get organized, find and train staff, and identify and claim all the properties that had been unlawfully seized. I called on the US Military Governor, General Lucius Clay, with a request to extend the deadline. But the General's main concern was that Soviet troops might try to take over all of Berlin and possibly all of Germany. (US personnel were even required to keep provisions in the trunk of their cars, in case emergency evacuation was ordered.) Clay explained that the sooner the restitution program was out of the way, the better. He was, understandably, opposed to any extension.

I argued that a massive search-and-claim operation would require immediate cash for German staff and equipment, and I asked for a grant from occupation funds to enable me to meet the rigid goal set in the military law. Clay noted that the German currency, which the occupying allied forces used to pay their own local expenses in Germany, were all under combined control of the four victorious powers. He was sure that the Soviets would never agree to such use, since they didn't believe in private ownership of property anyway. He doubted if the British or French would agree either, since they had not yet enacted similar restitution laws for their zones. It looked rather hopeless.

I proposed to Clay that instead of the grant, which would not be approved, he could give me a loan of German Marks from the US share of occupation funds. It would not require the consent of the others, and I could repay the loan when restitution funds were recovered. Clay asked if that could be done legally. I replied that I had in my pocket a memorandum that said it could. He ordered that the sizeable sum of one million marks was to be advanced, and I raced away to get started.

Under supervision of a small cadre of refugee Jewish lawyers, we hired German staff and sent them to scour every real-estate registry for every property transfer after 1933 by anyone with a name that sounded Jewish. Military Government law required persons who acquired Jewish property during the Hitler years to report the transfer. I requisitioned Army jeeps and a large hall that was used as a recreational center by Baltic nationals, many of whom had been Nazi collaborators. A pool of JRSO typists worked round the clock to hammer out the claims that poured in from the investigators in the field. In the final hours before the deadline, we packed a US Army Ambulance with over 163,000 claims and rushed them off to the official filing center. I phoned General Clay to tell him that no extension was needed. I think I gained his confidence on all restitution problems thereafter. I don't think I gained many friends among the Balts.

There is a sequel to this story that occurred years later, but perhaps should be recited here. The million mark loan approved by General Clay, although a considerable sum at the time, was soon spent. Shortly thereafter, East Berlin and East Germany were politically severed from the West – the cold war was on. General Clay was replaced by a Harvard-trained lawyer named John J. McCloy.

McCloy's assignment was to tie West Germany firmly into the fold of democratic nations. He recognized that what Germany did in the field of restitution would play an important role in her acceptance back among nations. McCloy was key in persuading German Chancellor Konrad Adenauer and others in the West German government to do whatever was possible to meet the compensation demands of Israel and Nazi victims.

I went to see McCloy, now the US High Commissioner of Germany, to explain that the money advanced by General Clay's authority had already been spent. I told him some money was coming in and being distributed to the victims of Nazi persecution. But aid was urgently needed to help concentration camp survivors move out of the Displaced Persons camps, a goal shared by both Germans and Americans. It would be politically and morally untenable, I argued, to give priority to the wrongdoers by returning borrowed funds to the now prospering German State while its victims remained in such desperate need. McCloy agreed. He approved a loan of another million marks to the JRSO.

The same moral arguments prevailed again when the loan was renewed, now for 3 million marks. Then came a moment of truth and opportunity. Among the defendants convicted as war criminals in Nuremberg was the industrialist Alfred Krupp, found guilty of seizure of foreign properties and use of concentration camp inmates as slave laborers. He was sentenced to 12 years in prison, and to the forfeit of all of his property. In 1958, as part of the general humanitarian review of all of the Nuremberg sentences, Krupp's sentence was reduced to time served, and all of his property was restored to him by order of McCloy. During my frequent contact with the High Commissioner, I had resisted the pressures of the Jewish organizations to try to influence McCloy's clemency decisions. I respected McCloy and recognized that he was struggling with a difficult matter of personal conscience. Now I could no longer remain silent.

After his ruling on Krupp, I went to his office in Bonn and reminded him of the JRSO loans of three million marks for restitution work. If he insisted, I would repay those loans in full. But I told him: 'I think that would be morally wrong. It should not be the victims who bear the expense of recovering only a portion of what was stolen from them. It should be at the expense of the wrongdoers.' Since he had just returned the assets of a convicted war criminal, worth probably more than three billion marks, I asked him to cancel the debt 'owed' by the victims of Nazi persecution. McCloy listened somberly and paused. 'Can I do that legally?' I told him: 'I have a memo in my pocket that says you can.' McCloy looked up and said, 'The debt is cancelled.'

Years later, when McCloy had passed his 90th birthday and was recording his memoirs, I saw him in New York and I reminded him of the JRSO debt cancellation story. The next day he phoned me: 'You know I might have gone to jail for that!' 'I know,' I replied, 'but I would have gone with you.' We both laughed, knowing we had done the right thing.

Retrieving Sacred Treasures

HITLER'S ANTI-SEMITIC 'INTELLECTUAL' Minister Alfred Rosenberg was responsible for assembling and preserving Jewish cultural objects that could prove the perfidy of the Jewish race, religion and ideology. In the Eastern territories overrun by Germany, Rosenberg collected Jewish torahs, religious ceremonial decorations, prayer books, and other sacred texts and objects. Much of this material was eventually stored in a large warehouse in Wiesbaden that came under the control of the US Military Government. The JRSO was entrusted with responsibility for the legal and equitable distribution of the captured booty. Of course, I had no experience whatsoever with the disposition of such artifacts.

It was obvious that stolen assets should be returned to their former owners. But that was easier said than done. In most cases, the former owners had been murdered by Nazi extermination programs, and the Jewish congregations were no longer in existence. What were we going to do? We concluded that we would do the best we could, but to those who saw these materials as holy, that may not have been good enough. It posed challenges of faith versus reason that could have stumped even Solomon or Maimonides who wrote a famous book to guide the perplexed.

Dispatching the Torahs was relatively easy. Many of them could be identified as coming from well-known synagogues in Poland, Lithuania, Latvia, Estonia, Ukraine, and other centers of Jewish learning. Where there was still a functioning synagogue in a particular area, Torahs were shipped back to their former congregations. But that was rare. Most Jewish communities in the East had been totally destroyed. Most survivors had sought a new life in Israel where the Ministry of Religion was happy to distribute the needed scrolls. A refugee community starting a new congregation in a strange land also received the rescued tablets of Jewish law.

Many of the Torahs, however, were damaged. I soon learned that a damaged Torah cannot be used in prayer. If the name of the Lord, as printed on the sacred parchment, has been damaged in any way, no repair is permissible. The Torah must be sent to Israel for burial in accordance with ancient Hebrew rituals. Other repairs are possible, but only by orthodox Jewish scribes. So we arranged to have a group of scribes come from Israel to work under the supervision of the respected American Joint Distribution Committee ('The Joint') offices in Paris. In one of my frequent visits to the Paris office, I encountered another problem that was rather perplexing.

We maintained strict inventory controls. Torahs were valuable. Every Torah coming in and going out had to be accounted for. Unfortunately, there was no computerized accounting available at that time, and security was not as tight as it should have been. I thought I detected a discrepancy in the number of Torahs we shipped to Paris and the number distributed or on hand. To ascertain the facts and confirm my suspicions would require a detailed examination – particularly of the orthodox scribes who had access to the sacred scrolls. That could prove to be very embarrassing. Besides, what would we do if we found that an old rabbi from Israel had pinched a Torah or two?

So I turned to the learned rabbi in charge of the operation (who was not completely beyond suspicion) and told him that I had a problem. I said I suspected that some of the Torahs may have disappeared, and I didn't know whether purloining a Torah was a blessed act or a criminal offense. I asked, 'Do I have to look up to heaven or down to the Devil to find the culprit?' He replied in Yiddish, 'Do not look up or down – take my advice – kik vek!' (Look away!) I learned from that rabbi that sometimes the best thing to do may be to do nothing.

Not all rabbis adopted so benign an approach. When dealing with the captured ceremonial objects such as candelabra, silver plates, wine goblets, Torah crowns, and all of the related paraphernalia used in a variety of Jewish rituals and holidays, we followed the same basic principles. Wherever possible, we tried to identify and locate the former owner and return the property. If it was damaged, we tried to repair it. This was sometimes even more difficult than repairing a scroll. Missing parts of ceremonial objects could be scattered among several different boxes. The experts we brought from Israel's Bezalel Museum, two fine gentlemen named Shunami and Narkiss, searched long and diligently, trying to restore every object. In the end there were many broken pieces, including table silver and broken candlesticks, which were beyond repair and had to be considered as scrap metal. After long deliberation, in which other members of my executive staff participated, we thought we had found a good solution.

We shipped these broken bits of scrap silver to England to the well-reputed smelting company run by the Jewish Goldsmith family. They were instructed to melt down the objects so that the proceeds could be distributed by 'The Joint' and the Jewish Agency for Israel to the most needy Nazi survivors. Soon thereafter, I sailed for New York to make my annual report to the JRSO Board of Directors. I was confident that I might receive their praise and possibly also their blessing. I learned that one should not count one's blessings too soon.

I proudly reported to the Board about the work done in recovering Jewish properties, homes, businesses, art works, Torah scrolls, and silver ceremonial objects that had been returned to owners or made available to needy congregations. Board members smiled happily at the thought that they had vicariously participated in such noble work. I then detailed what had been done with the smelted scrap silver. Before I was quite through, a hand was being waved furiously by Rabbi Isaac Lewin, the respected head of the orthodox Union of American Hebrew Congregations. He rose slowly and said, his voice trembling, 'Do my ears believe me? Did I hear you say that you took these sacred Jewish objects, the last remnant of our murdered ancestors, and you sent them to a CREMATORIUM??' There was silence. Stunned, I stuttered that we had done the best we could under the circumstances. It was only many years later that I felt I had been forgiven by the Rabbi.

There was another incident regarding sacred treasures. A Jewish US Army Chaplain had apparently raided the warehouse in which the Germans had stored the most valuable Jewish religious books. Being a man who obviously believed in restitution, the Captain had backed an army ambulance up to the warehouse and filled it with Nazi loot. He arranged to ship it to Israel on a refugee ship – probably also illegal – as a brave gesture of retaliatory justice.

It turned out that many of the volumes had belonged to an anti-Nazi Christian sect (I believe it was the Templars) who had acquired the sacred tomes lawfully long before the Nazis came to power. They wanted their property back. General Clay summoned me and ordered that since I was in charge of Jewish restitution, I had better get those ancient books restituted back to their rightful non-Jewish anti-Nazi owners. He gave me a long list of the missing volumes. I promised to do the best I could.

On my next trip to Israel, I raised the issue with government representatives. They were apologetic and promised to redress the situation. But the books by then had been sent to the Hebrew University on Mt. Scopus, and unfortunately, that territory was in Arab hands. They promised to correct the error as soon as the military situation allowed. I reported the facts to General Clay. Nothing more could be done. What finally happened to the books, I do not know. I hope they were restored. 'Kik vek', Don't ask!

Reclaiming Cemeteries

IT CAME ABOUT that, by early 1949, I became the custodian of several hundred Jewish cemeteries located throughout the Federal Republic of Germany. They fell into the category of properties previously owned by Jewish congregations that had been dissolved by Nazi decree. By virtue of the US Military Government restitution law, now the lawful titleholder was the Jewish Restitution Successor Organization. The truth is, never having been an occupant thereof, I was ignorant about the management of cemeteries. So to my relief, I managed to persuade three distinguished rabbinical scholars, including the Chief Rabbi of Israel, to advise me on all religious practices and prohibitions concerning such holy plots.

Little did I realize what lay in store. First, it was essential to learn precisely what was permissible or impermissible regarding the ancient burial grounds for religious congregations that no longer existed. It was not something taught in my Property class at Harvard. My rabbinical council made clear that very special rules apply: once a cemetery, always a cemetery; no flowers can be placed on the casket or grave; if a tombstone falls, it must be left lying where it fell; nothing can ever be done to profane the bodies or memory of the deceased. Honoring these ancient traditions seemed simple enough, but it soon became apparent that dealing with the dead can make life quite complicated for the living.

The ancient German city of Fulda is noted for its large Benedictine Abbey that for centuries helped spread Christianity throughout the land. Catholic Bishops met there regularly to honor the memory of St. Boniface who is buried in its beautiful baroque cathedral. Although Jews had lived in Fulda for many generations, their burial grounds were not nearly as impressive. Soon after the Nazis came to power in Germany in 1933, they completely desecrated the old Jewish cemetery. Following Hilter's defeat, a new Jewish community, a handful of refugees from Eastern Europe, again took root there. Mortuary records revealed that a sizeable area of the cemetery had never been used. Since it seemed unlikely that it would ever be needed by the few Jewish settlers in Fulda, the question arose whether the unused grounds could be sold to raise funds for needy survivors.

Of course, I referred the question to the rabbinical council. The answer came back that an area that never contained any bodies could not be considered a cemetery. If a wall could be erected to enclose the former burial grounds then the unoccupied portion outside the wall might be sold, providing it was not used for any profane purpose. As the former victims needed money desperately, we were pleased when the local government expressed an interest in purchasing the available unused land. City authorities wanted to build a new customs office and were willing to build a little park on the desecrated site and add a plaque commemorating those who had perished.

Hardly a year had passed when I received an alarming telegram in New York. A story had appeared in the German press that, while digging the foundations for the new custom house in Fulda, a number of bones had been found. They were presumed to be of Jews. I cabled to seek an immediate injunction to stop all construction and took the next plane back to Germany.

At a meeting with the local Jewish community leaders and the officials of the city of Fulda, it appeared that the contract had been violated. Having recently prosecuted ss leaders who had murdered over a million Jews, I was in no mood to tolerate the desecration of Jewish graves. I demanded that the building, which was already five stories high and near completion, be torn down immediately and the area restored.

The leaders of the new Jewish community in Fulda asked to speak with me privately. They implored me not to take such a harsh position. They noted that they had to live in Fulda, that the city officials were anti-Nazis who had been most accommodating to the new Jewish settlers, that it was only a small area that had been trespassed, and there was even no certainty that the bones that had been dug up belonged to humans. They argued that their lives in Fulda would be made unbearable if I forced the city to tear down the expensive building. I reluctantly agreed to refer the entire file to the rabbinical council in Jerusalem for its recommendation.

The three learned scholars cited the provisions of the Talmud about respecting the memory and body of the dead, noting particularly that no building of any kind could be placed on top of a Jewish cemetery. They suggested that it would be acceptable if the building could be elevated so that it did not touch the holy ground. How that was to be done was not made clear. It was obvious that the Talmud did not teach engineering. Since no one knew how to raise a five story building, a second opinion seemed called for. To this day, I do not know which brilliant mind gave birth to the solution.

The genius who found the answer noted that only one type of structure was permissible on a Jewish cemetery, namely a chapel where prayers for the dead could be said. There was apparently nothing in the Talmud that prohibited any structure on top of such a chapel. If therefore, a chapel could be built under the part of the building that trespassed on the old cemetery, that part of the building would not rest on the cemetery itself, but only on the roof of a new little synagogue in the cellar. Since that would be Kosher – so to speak – that's exactly what we did.

So under a corner of the Zollamt, a dignified triangular room was built, no larger than about 15 feet in any direction. A Hebrew inscription adorns the wall. Small stained glass windows near the ceiling provide a strained glimpse of the parking lot. Above it stands a monumental five-story office building. None of the drivers who park their cars on the parking lot have any idea that they are placing their vehicle on the roof of a holy place.

About 10 years later, I saw it again. At the customs house, an elderly gent with a jangling a bunch of keys, introduced himself and explained that he had been there when the building was constructed. Yes, there was indeed a Jewish prayer room in the cellar. He led me out to the parking lot, and then down some steps... He kicked away some cardboard cartons blocking the entrance and unlocked the heavy door. Lo and behold – there was my little synagogue, a bit dusty but quite intact. I asked him if anyone had every visited the room since it was built. 'Not to my knowledge,' he said.

If you ever visit Fulda, ask for the old Zollamt. Beneath a large office building that was the old customs house you may find the smallest and most unknown and unused Jewish prayer house in the world. It shall remain in perpetuity as a tribute to Jewish creativity or ingenuity – or something.

Not too long thereafter, I attended a meeting in Bonn with representatives of the West German Finance Ministry and the Ministry of Social Affairs. I was joined by Dr. Ernst Katzenstein, one of my deputies. The main item on the agenda was to reach an accord regarding the care and maintenance of unused Jewish cemeteries.

Municipalities in Germany traditionally provide burial plots for their local inhabitants in a municipal cemetery. Every citizen has the right to be buried there and to have a tombstone of limited size over the grave. Municipal burials take place next to each other in chronological sequence. After 20 years, the stone must be removed and the same plot is made available for newcomers. Jewish burial practices are more sentimental, less orderly, and more enduring. It might have been anticipated that these differences would lead to a clash.

When discussions commenced, the German negotiators were polite and friendly. They readily acknowledged that their predecessor government was responsible for the fact that Jewish cemeteries were burned and desecrated, and that many Jewish communities that had existed in Germany for centuries had disappeared. They were prepared, within their means as a divided nation that had been impoverished and ruined by war, to see that the grass was cut and the Jewish graves tended in areas where the Jews were all gone. They would receive the same benefits and rights that were accorded to their own German gravesites. Obviously, they had never read the Talmud.

Katzenstein expressed appreciation, but I explained that the Jewish tradition called for the maintenance of a Jewish cemetery not only for 20 years, but in perpetuity. They rebutted quietly with the argument that we couldn't really expect the German taxpayers to assume an indefinite burden for Jews that they didn't even give to their own German citizens. That did it. I exploded! The wrath of Ferencz was upon them!

I shouted at them that if they hadn't murdered the Jews and driven them out, they would not have any problem with Jewish cemeteries. It was only because of the horrendous Nazi crimes that the subject had to be discussed. I pulled from my pocket a small packet of bones I had picked up in the grass at Auschwitz and slammed them on the table. Shaking with anger, I screamed, 'Who shall pay? Shall these pay? Then you go and ask them!' Katzenstein, fearing that we would come to blows, ran from the room. The Chairman called a recess. I cannot recall any other time in my life when I gave way to such an outburst of anger. It was unjustified. Our negotiating partners were not the ones who committed the crimes, and I regretfully do not recall that I even offered an apology. When the parties reassembled, some 20 minutes later, the German representatives quietly said that they would accept the obligation to honor the Jewish traditions. That meant that the former Jewish cemeteries would be cared for and maintained at the German government's expense forever.

Bulk Settlements for Property Claims

RECOVERING STOLEN JEWISH assets as prescribed by the Military Government law was a complicated legal process. Wherever possible, JRSO lawyers would seek a quick cash settlement with the possessor of property subject to restitution. But that was rarely possible. In the absence of a negotiated amicable accord, the claim would be decided by a special panel of German judges, almost all of whom had been members of the Nazi Party. Their decision could be appealed to a regular German court, then to a superior German tribunal, and from there to the final Supreme Restitution Court then composed of American judges. Those who were ordered to surrender properties they had acquired from Jews during the Nazi period were lawfully entitled to get back what they had paid – but there was a problem. The original Reichsmark that had been paid were now worthless. A new currency reform law proclaimed that one new Deutsche mark would be valued as the equivalent of ten of the old Reichmark. The acquirers of Jewish property wanted to get back one Deutsche mark for every Reichmark they had paid. Who should bear the loss caused by the devaluation of the currency was a hotly debated legal and moral issue.

The 'Aryanizers' of Jewish property almost invariably argued that they had paid a fair price, had paid off mortgages, had made many repairs, or were purchasers in good faith. They felt they were being unfairly hounded by this strange American-Jewish organization and its Director-General. Old anti-Semitic roots were being watered. Although we won every case in the Court of Restitution Appeals, it became clear that we needed to find a more expeditious and less contentious way to achieve our goals.

We hit upon a plan that might get us out of our difficult and time-consuming dilemma. If the German State governments could be persuaded to 'buy' all of the Jewish Restitution Successor Organization claims for a fair price, there would be no unjust enrichment on their part, and we would have immediate cash on hand to carry out our urgent charitable obligations. The German authorities could then take their time and make whatever concessions to their citizens that they felt were equitable. It took long negotiations to persuade state governments to accept the principle of a 'global settlement'. Difficult appraisals had to be made regarding the fair value of thousands of properties before agreement could be reached. Since the plan offered benefits to all parties concerned, a deal was finally struck. It was a most novel and creative solution to a difficult political problem.

The first state government to accept the arrangement for a quick cash payment was the State of Hesse. They would pay the Jewish successor organization 25 million marks in cash. That was a lot of money at that time. Arrangements were made to have the formal contract signing in a splendid royal house situated in the midst of a beautiful park in the state capital at Wiesbaden. This would be the first time that any post-Hitler official was to enter into a settlement of claims with an organization representing the 'world Jewry' that Hitler sought to destroy. Other States were expected to follow the example. It was to be a solemn and momentous occasion, symbolic of a new relationship between Germany and the Jews.

I asked my Deputy, Dr. Ernst Katzenstein, to join me for the signing ceremonies. He had fled from Germany to England and Israel before joining the JRSO. I packed the heap of legal papers into a new attaché case I had recently bought in the US Army PX. It was a neat box bound in beautiful red leather and carrying it made me feel like a British Prime Minister. Katzenstein was impressed and bought an identical one for himself. He agreed to join me and to stay over in Wiesbaden to do some work at our regional office in the area. We would proceed together by car to the Royal Palace for the auspicious historical event.

When we arrived there, we were greeted by a welcoming party. I conspicuously branded the beautiful red attaché case as I placed it on the large round table in the pompous conference room. The Minister President made the first speech, noting the importance of the special occasion. The Finance

Minister and the Justice Minister also made appropriate remarks heralding the event. Then it was my turn. I made some observations about how happy I was that we had finally reached the point of signing such a historic and important document on behalf of Nazi victims. I then reached for the contract in my beautiful red attaché case. I snapped it open with verve. Out popped Katzenstein's pajamas!

A Treaty to Compensate Victims

HOW, WITH WHAT method and means does one begin to heal the wounds of those who bore the brunt of the crimes perpetrated by the vicious Hitler regime?

Early in 1951, the new State of Israel called upon the four Occupying Powers to seek compensation for victims of Nazi oppression. There was no response from the Allies or the Germans. West Germany's Chancellor, Konrad Adenauer, was eager to restore his country to the family of civilized nations. He was a devout Catholic whom the Nazis had driven out of office as the Mayor of Cologne. He had escaped further persecution with the help of a Jewish friend. Mindful of Israel's appeal, Adenauer publicly acknowledged that unspeakable crimes had been committed in the name of the German people, and that imposed on them an obligation to make amends. The President of the World Jewish Congress, Nahum Goldmann, formerly of Berlin, responded to Adenauer's overture by calling a conference in New York of the world's leading Jewish organizations. I was invited to attend as an 'expert', which Goldmann defined as 'one who knows everything, but nothing else'.

The conference took place in a large New York hotel. Representatives of all the major national and international Jewish groups were present. What was scheduled as a meeting to discuss reconciliation soon turned into a battleground. The doors were forced open and a large group of young men, many with flowing curls under their skull caps, stormed into the room. They brandished placards and shouted at the delegates to disperse since they were disgracing Jewish honor by talking about taking blood money from murderers. I thought of the parable of Jesus chasing his money-changing brethren from the synagogue. I recall one of the delegates, a rabbi, cringing under a table. There was no need for him to fear. With the help of a few Irish cops, the intruders were firmly escorted from the room.

The very idea of sitting down with Germans to discuss money in connection with the Holocaust understandably gave rise to emotional outbursts on all sides. The Israeli Parliament in Jerusalem was stoned when the subject was raised. Many Knesset members were convinced that negotiating with Germans would lead only to more betrayals. Ben Gurion, Israel's Prime Minister, passed the hot potato to Goldmann. In the end, all agreed that it would be immoral and unwise to reject Adenauer's overture and expression of repentance.

What emerged was a new Jewish non-profit organization, incorporated in New York under the peculiar title 'The Conference on Jewish Material Claims Against Germany (Claims Conference)'. There was general agreement that no agreement would be reached without the partnership of Israel, which had given refuge to so many of Hitler's victims. A later meeting in London set the agenda for the negotiations between the new German government and representatives of the Jewish organizations. I was invited to join the group.

For a full week, we labored in Grosvenor House drafting statements and proposals. Moses Leavitt, Executive of the respected American Joint Distribution Committee, played a leading role. The negotiations were very difficult and painful. Does one ask for compensation for the six million Jews murdered? How much is one human life worth? How do you measure or prove degrees of fear, or pain, or suffering? I never found such questions in my law books at Harvard. None of us were prepared to put a price tag on any human life.

We finally reached agreements on the outlines of what could be presented as valid legal claims. Incarceration in a concentration camp, for example, was illegal deprivation of liberty – its duration could be measured and verified. Physical disability caused by persecution could also be translated into measurable financial terms. Other economic losses could also be calculated. Compensation would be demanded for three distinct categories of claims: first and foremost for still-undefined personal injuries; next would be a global sum to the State of Israel to reimburse the costs of rehabilitating survivors; lastly, a sum would have to be given to the Claims Conference for ongoing relief of Nazi victims outside of Israel.

Because of antipathy among many Jews to anything German, and the tension furthered by militant Jewish groups, it was agreed that negotiations should not take place in Germany and should be kept secret. It was 'leaked' that the Claims Conference delegation would fly by special plane to a meeting in Brussels. That posed a special problem for me. Not too long before, my wife and I had bailed out of a disabled plane over the ruins of Berlin. The trauma of that parachuting incident left my wife gravely concerned every time I had to get into a plane. My colleagues were aware of the problem. Israeli Security agents responsible for our safety informed me to follow instructions that I would receive in a sealed envelope when I checked out of the London hotel. In the cab, I opened the envelope, which read: 'Proceed to Hoek van Holland. You'll be met.'

I got to the English coast as soon as I could, and took the channel ferry to 'The Hoek'. When I presented my passport, a man in a dark suit appeared with a black Buick sedan. He whisked me off into the darkness. As dawn was breaking, I asked him who he was and where he was taking me. He replied politely that he was with the Dutch Security Police and was taking me to the meeting site. I tried to doze until I noticed that the car had turned off on to small roads and was proceeding very slowly. Half-awake, I was suddenly startled to find the car surrounded by what I thought were uniformed ss men with dogs. My memory flashed back to the concentration camps where I had last seen such guards, and my heart pounded in fear that I had fallen into an ss trap. Then I noticed, as the car pulled through the gate, that the men in black uniforms with black boots did not have the ss Death Head insignia on their collar. The Dutch Police uniform was remarkably similar to that worn by the German ss – my fears were unjustified.

During the meetings, we were being carefully guarded by the Dutch and Israeli Security Services. We were warned not to open any suspicious parcels or envelopes. A letter bomb had been sent to Professor Franz Boehm, the head of the German delegation. It had been intercepted and defused. Earlier, a bomb placed in a hollowed-out German encyclopedia addressed to Chancellor Adenauer had killed two policemen in Munich. A plane carrying two delegates from Israel exploded on landing at Frankfurt airport. We learned that a gang of Jewish 'terrorists' had entered Holland with plans to kill all those who disgraced Jewish honor. Menachin Begin, who later became Prime Minister, was reportedly the leader of one of the terrorist gangs.

One day, in the midst of negotiations, an Israeli Security agent came up behind me and whispered that I was wanted outside. I excused myself, and another Security guard gingerly showed me a soiled envelope. He asked if I recognized the handwriting of the sender. I said, 'Of course,' as I ripped it open and the guards jumped away. It was a letter from my wife in Nuremberg. She enclosed two strips of antacid pills to help ease my tensions and two rows of film taken of our two infant children. Security had detected the powders and the strips of celluloid and concluded that it might be a letter-bomb. They soaked it in oil or did some other mysterious thing before they dared hand it to me. Instead of being blown up, we all had a needed laugh.

After about six months of difficult negotiations, we reached agreement. The signing ceremony was scheduled to take place in Luxembourg, where Chancellor Adenauer had scheduled other meetings. First, the accord had to be initialed by the heads of the German and Claims Conference delegations. I picked up Professor Franz Boehm, and my driver drove us from Frankfurt to The Hague where Leavitt, who was ailing, initialed for the Claims Conference. We proceeded immediately toward Luxembourg. Our route took us through Bastogne in Belgium that I had last seen during the Battle of the Bulge when the town was almost completely destroyed. I guessed we could find a cafe open. In the middle of the night we stopped at an inn for coffee. I told the Belgian owner that I had been one of the US soldiers who had liberated the town from the Germans. Now we were escorting a German official trying to reach out for reconciliation with Nazi victims and Israel. The Belgian café owner absolutely refused to accept any payment for the refreshments.

The Reparations Treaty was signed in Luxembourg on the morning of September 10, 1952. Chancellor Adenauer, who was to sign first, discovered that his pen had run out of ink. A bad omen? I handed Goldmann a pen that my wife had given to me when I graduated from law school in 1943. It was an old Watermann with a lifetime guarantee. Whose life was guaranteed, it didn't say. She gave it to me as a good luck charm with a promise that I would return with it after the war. I had carried it with me safely through every campaign. Goldmann handed it across the table to Adenauer and said he would be honored if the Chancellor signed with 'his' pen. I demanded restitution from Goldmann after the meeting. That historic pen will join my archives at the US Holocaust Museum in Washington.

Seeking Fair Compensation – A Mission Impossible

THE TREATY THAT was signed on September 10, 1952, was frequently referred to as a 'Reparations Agreement', which it wasn't. That term usually applies to nations that have been at war. It was also known as the 'Hague Agreement' though it was signed in Luxembourg. Some called it the 'Luxembourg Agreement', but Luxembourg had nothing to do with it. The Israelis referred to it as the 'Shilumim Agreement', which no one who didn't speak Hebrew understood. In fact, none of the signatories had any reasonable conception of the magnitude of the obligations involved in the treaty they had just solemnly signed. It was the product of political considerations cloaked in moral garb, and heralded as a solution to some profound human and legal problems that, in fact, could never be resolved.

Negotiations for compensation would not have started without prior secret assurances, given by Konrad Adenauer to Nahum Goldmann, that Germany was prepared to make a significant payment. A billion was a nice round minimum figure that Goldmann liked, even though it was never quite certain whether he had in mind dollars or German marks that were worth only half as much. It did not take very long for West Germany to agree to pay Israel one and a half billion dollars – but they didn't have the money. Instead of cash, payments would be spread out over 10 to 12 years and would be in the form of German goods. That ingenious arrangement would serve to prime the German economic pump while enabling Israel to use or sell the goods. It was an ironic twist of fate that railroad trains and taxicabs, as well as many other necessities for the first Jewish State, came from the country that sought to annihilate the Jews.

The parties further agreed that another half-billion dollars in goods would be supplied to the Claims Conference to carry out its relief work for Nazi victims outside of Israel. The most important part of the deal was the cash compensation that would be made directly to those individuals who had personally endured the brunt of Nazi persecution. Since there were no provisions in the normal German law, or the law of any other country, to deal with payments for such atrocities, special legislation would be required to achieve the stated goals. What was needed was a new Federal Indemnification Law that would pass muster by both the upper and lower houses of the German Bundestag and be supported by the German public. The responsibility for negotiating the details of this legislation with the German government was assigned to a Claims Conference Legal Committee, of which I was a part. No one present had any experience in such matters, and none of us had any idea how it would turn out.

The most serious losses and injuries never came within the purview of the new law. About six million Jews had been murdered in cold blood by Hitler's eager executioners. Gypsies suffered a similar fate, as did many other opponents of the Hitler regime, including many Germans. No one on the Jewish side ever suggested that any payment should be requested, or accepted, for this senseless genocide. When this issue was first discussed at our preparatory meetings in London, it was recognized that we should not try to place any monetary value on a human life. It was just too painful to consider whether papa was more valuable than grandma or a baby sister. Most of us had tears in our eyes when we discussed it. Nor could we measure the pain of a survivor who saw his family being murdered, or the constant fear of camp inmates who had been threatened with imminent beatings and death. Such sufferings were beyond the reach of specification, comprehension, or compensation. The Claims Conference title referred only to 'material claims'. We were trying to fit into a legal frame some measure of redress based on concepts developed among civilized people accustomed to civilized behavior. The crimes of the Holocaust could not be pressed into such a mould. Blinded by outrage and the desperate needs of impoverished survivors who cried out for justice, we embarked on a mission impossible.

Implementing Compensation Agreements

MANY OF THE committee members, who were expected to protect overall Jewish interests, seemed to focus primarily on serving their own constituents. Those who had been employees of the pre-Hitler civil service demanded reinstatements of all their lost entitlements. Those who had resettled in Germany wanted support for the new communities. Yiddish-speaking Jews from Eastern Europe were viewed as interlopers by some of their 'enlightened' German brethren. Even those who had escaped from behind the Iron Curtain showed little concern for those who had been left behind. Since I had no personal axe to grind, I was often forced into the role of mediator among our own so-called 'legal experts' in order to present to the world a picture of unity among the disunited Jewish representatives.

As to the German negotiators, many who were carryovers from the former regime did not feel any moral or legal obligation to impose onerous costs on patriotic German taxpayers who had loyally supported their government. That's what all good citizens are expected to do in time of war, isn't it? The conservative Finance Minister, Fritz Schaeffer, relied heavily upon the simple argument that Jewish demands exceeded Germany's capacity to pay. Powerful holders of bonds issued by the Third Reich demanded priority payment, insisting that there could be no economic recovery without restoring Germany's credit. Beneficiaries competed for a bigger slice of the meager pie. Vague compromises were hammered out in a hurry. The new Federal Indemnification Law – the *Bundesentschädigungsgesetz* (BEG), which non-Germans could neither spell nor pronounce – was enacted in October

1953. It stipulated that the program for compensating Nazi victims would be completed within ten years. (Fifty years later, after $ 50 billion dollars had been paid out to more than 500,000 survivors, a reunited Germany was planning a new foundation to wrap up their indemnification responsibilities.)

As soon as the West German government enacted the new indemnification law, all victims of Nazi persecution became entitled to claim compensation for a large variety of injuries and losses. It was clear to me that claimants would need legal assistance to submit and prove the validity of their claims. The Jewish Restitution Successor Organization dealt only with the recovery of heirless properties. The Claims Conference was responsible for negotiating the details of new German compensation laws. But who would help the victims file and prove the validity of their unprecedented claims? Jewish claimants could not be expected to turn to a former Nazi lawyer for help or be able to pay for legal assistance.

Moses Leavitt, executive head of 'The Joint', recognized that a new organization was needed to help the claimants. After all, if camp survivors received compensation, their need for charitable help would be diminished. 'Moe' Leavitt was better known as 'No Leavitt' because of his tight-fisted monetary controls. Since I was already head of the JRSO and Claims Conference offices in Germany, he concluded that I was just the right man to organize and direct a United Restitution Organization (URO) to provide legal aid to needy claimants. All the reins would then be in one hand and that would ensure uniformity of policies. No increase in my meager salary was considered necessary.

To provide legal assistance to claimants for a modest contingent fee, URO offices were opened wherever there were large numbers of former Nazi victims who might need help in submitting claims. Eventually, there were URO branches in 19 countries, and offices in the major cities of Germany where special Finance Ministry agencies dealt with the indemnification claims. Hundreds of thousands of claims poured in. Each one had to be accompanied by persuasive evidence. Medical examinations had to be translated and verified. The German agencies were swamped with literally millions of claims from Jews as well as non-Jews. German nationals and non-Jews were also among Hitler's victims, and they all benefited from the legislation pushed by the Claims Conference.

In many cases, it was almost impossible to prove the direct causal connection between the alleged injury and the persecution. Despite the best efforts of the URO staff of over 1,000 persons, including 250 carefully screened German lawyers, practically all of the claimants had one thing in common: they all felt that whatever they got was too little and too late. With angry complaints, they blamed the URO. A common complaint was that everybody else had already been paid, or had received more for the same injuries. What claimants did not realize was that a reasonably competent and underpaid staff was working very hard to get as much as possible for them. Some German agencies were sympathetic, but many were antagonistic. They were required by law to be meticulous, and there was no way to deal with so many complicated claims in a short period of time. Protracted litigation was often unavoidable.

I recall the head of the URO office in Stockholm phoning me in a panic about the clients rioting in the office. I told him to convene a meeting of all the complainers in the main synagogue, and I would be there on the next plane. I took off my jacket when I addressed the unruly crowd. I took their complaints in English, German, French, Hungarian, and Yiddish. Then I invited anyone who felt he could get better service elsewhere to please come to the office in the morning, and we would be happy to give him or her their file back with our best wishes. Of course, not a single complainer showed up.

One of the loudest complaints by the Displaced Persons (DPs) who remained in Germany was that the directors of the Jewish restitution organizations traveled in American sedans. 'Look at them riding around in big cars with 'unser gelt' – 'our money'!' What the disgruntled complainers did not know was that originally I obtained cars, and maintenance, without charge from the US military. When that dried up, I purchased cars from soldiers who were being transferred back to the US. The vehicles would later be sold, and usually at a profit. Transportation by car was the most efficient and cheapest way to get around to the scattered restitution offices. Rather than being a spendthrift at the expense of the survivors, the Director-General often found himself in the role of a used car salesman.

Many DPs fleeing anti-semitism in Poland and other Eastern countries fled to Germany where they took up residence. They argued that the former Jewish communal property like synagogues, schools, or old-age homes now belonged to them. The issue of ownership of the communal properties, and properties of organizations that had been dissolved by Nazi decree, finally came before the US Court of Restitution Appeals. The legal arguments took place in the courthouse at Nuremberg where the war crimes trials had been held. I told the American judges sadly that I had stood on the same spot when I prosecuted Nazi murderers of the Jews, and I never thought that I would stand there again to argue against a Jewish congregation. My legal responsibilities under the restitution law were not merely to aid those now in Germany, but also the majority who had been forced to flee. The judges agreed. The landmark decision did not make me very popular with the new Jewish Communities, even though the JRSO had given the local Jewish communities everything they reasonably needed for their survival and growth.

One flamboyant German official, Philip Auerbach, in charge of compensation claims in Bavaria, was quite a bizarre figure. It was rumored that he had been interned by the Nazis because he was tainted by Jewish blood. It was known that he paid little attention to formalities. I always considered him neurotic. On several occasions he sought me out for a donation from the JRSO for some strange scheme he had concocted. I always refused. I recall a detailed plan he had for shipping Hitler's stolen art works to the US for exhibitions in museums that would pay well for the privilege. The money would then go back to the compensation fund. He had the name of the ship, the museums, and the amounts payable. I was not really surprised when, after I checked it out, I learned that it was all a figment of his imagination. When he and the head of a local Jewish community announced that they were establishing a Jewish Restitution Bank to receive deposits from concentration camp victims, I immediately cabled Jewish organizations throughout the world to beware. Exactly one year later, the police closed down the so-called bank; the finances of the Auerbach office were under investigation, and he committed suicide. It was a crazy time with crazy people doing crazy things.

Some Unanticipated Consequences

THE VARIETY AND unpredictability of the work in which we were engaged were unimaginable. All religious congregations in Germany are treated as official government entities. They are supported by income taxes levied on those who declare their religious affiliations. Nazi laws decreed that all Jewish organizations be dissolved, and their assets forfeited to the Reich. Rabbis, teachers, social workers, and even those responsible for circumcisions had to flee for their lives. During the course of the negotiations in The Hague, the question arose about who was to pay for the lost pensions of those Jewish officials. The German negotiators balked, saying they had no way to confirm which officials would have been entitled to what pension. Wearing my Claims Conference hat, I proposed that we cap the obligation at 30 million marks. They still refused. We countered with a proposal to set up a committee to certify each claim, and if the Social Ministry did not agree, no payment need be made. That was so reasonable that they dropped their objections. Then the fun began.

We set up a Pensions Advisory Board in a small office in Bonn in a rickety old building that was inexpensive because the landlord rented rooms by the hour. Our sole staff member, a very meticulous German Jew, E.G. Lowenthal, received the applications from former Jewish officials and, based on his own extensive knowledge and investigations, prepared the initial recommendations. The other Advisory Board members consisted of knowledgeable persons drawn from the JRSO, URO, and Claims Conference. I was Chairman, and my knowledge of the subject was practically nonexistent. Fortunately, the files were clear and comprehensive, and many claims could be rejected or approved with little discussion. In case there was a tie vote, I would always give the benefit of the doubt to the claimant. My ignorance was no excuse for rejecting an application.

Sometimes it was a very close judgment. I recall a case where it appeared that a particular rabbi was on the verge of being fired for cause – such as his occasional failure to appear at funerals because he may have been busy privately consoling the widow. Instead of a pension, his congregants were getting ready to give the rabbinical Romeo the boot. There were several cases where the negative decision of the Advisory Board was overruled by the Social Ministry that insisted on paying the claimant. In such cases, I felt that our Board had been too strict, and I felt better about approving the request of the loving rabbi whose congregation may not have been so forgiving. My greatest satisfaction came when it became apparent that the pensions program cost the German government at least ten times more than the 30 million marks I had offered to settle all pension claims. The only thing dumber than my proposal was Germany's rejection of it.

I should also mention the unsuccessful struggle to obtain compensation for Nazi victims from the communist government of the German Democratic Republic (GDR). For about 10 years, starting around 1974, as attorney for the Claims Conference, I conducted secret negotiations with representatives of the GDR in East Berlin. The US State Department was fully informed, and even offered to intervene if my efforts failed. I would pass through the border controls at Checkpoint Charley and proceed on foot to the US Embassy in East Berlin. Then I would meet the Antifascist Resistance Fighters, a front for the communist government. To be safe, I never took the taxi that was usually parked at the East German side of the divide. I always walked in the center of the street, facing the traffic, and avoided coming close to any doorways where someone might be lurking. I remembered my friend Charley Jordan of The Joint who was on a charitable mission in communist Prague and was later found floating in the river. His murderers were never apprehended.

Negotiations with the communist GDR were usually polite, but tense. My East German counterpart was a communist who had been interned in the Nazi concentration camp at Mauthausen. I had been with the American army when the camp was liberated. I told him that we were both acting as representatives of others, but since I had risked my life to save his, I hoped we could at least be honest with each other. He agreed.

The leaders of the GDR, having themselves been persecuted, felt no legal or moral obligation to compensate any other victim. After many sharp and often unpleasant meetings, I detected that the GDR was planning to do something. They requested the bank account number of the Claims Conference. I stalled and reported back to base. Goldmann sent word to call him in Paris if anything developed. The next day, as I entered the negotiation room in November 1976, there were liquor bottles and glasses on the table, and cameramen in the room. The GDR representative read a statement in the name of their 'Head of State' the gist of which was that the GDR was making a donation of one million dollars to the Claims Conference to benefit the needy Jews in the United States. They offered a toast. I replied that I would relay the message. I walked the half-mile back to the US Embassy and, from there, phoned Goldmann in Paris. I suggested that we thank them for this first installment, and continue the talks. Goldmann replied that it was like 'throwing the dog a bone'. He called a press conference and blasted the GDR. I got out of East Berlin as quickly as I could. It was rather a unique historic occasion when, about a week later, the Claims Conference sent a million dollar check back to the GDR.

No one anticipated that the initial indemnification law that was called for by the Reparations Agreement of September 1952, which led to the Indemnification Law of October 1953, would have to be expanded repeatedly over time. Additional special agreements were later reached with West Germany to close some of the undeniable holes in the compensation net. No one expected that communist East Germany would collapse as the cold war ended, and that there would be a unified Germany with complete independence from the former occupiers. By that time, my interest had moved away from seeking compensation for the Holocaust to trying to prevent another Holocaust. But that's another story.

Note

....

*   Adapted from website: www.benferencz.org

¶

ANTONIO CASSESE

Soliloquy[*]

My Early Years: Hesitating
between Law and Humanities

ANTONIO CASSESE

I READ LAW only because I was urged to do so by my father, a somewhat
impecunious historian who worked as a civil servant (he was director of the
local Public Record Office). I wanted to study philosophy or humanities.
We lived in a poor region of southern Italy (Campania), which was plagued
by unemployment, and my father's advice was that I should choose a field
that would ensure a secure professional future. I eventually enrolled at the
University of Pisa, primarily because in that central Italian town there was
a chance to enter a 'Juridical College' (associated, in those years, with the
celebrated Scuola Normale Superiore) that not only provided free board and
lodging, but also high-level training in addition to that imparted by the Pisa
Law School. Studying law proved tough for someone whose mind was set
rather on philosophy or sociology. But I learned the hard discipline of law.
Almost all the teachers were excellent, their method that of strict positivism. I thus absorbed the rigorous logical and systematic approach of that
method along with all the attendant technical tools of legal interpretation.
Still, I gradually came to feel attracted only to constitutional and international law, for they were less distant from political and social reality than,
say, torts, evidence, or commercial law. In the end, on personal grounds (the
professor of constitutional law was moving to Turin University and a new
professor of international law, Giuseppe Sperduti, had just been appointed),
I opted for international law. But there, again, I picked a rather unsophisti-
cated topic when it came to choosing a topic for my LLM dissertation: the
self-determination of peoples. In addition, I asked permission to study in
Germany, at Frankfurt am Main, and I spent a semester there, ostensibly
to research my thesis but in reality to attend lectures held by two leading
sociologists, Theodor Wiesengrund Adorno and Max Horkheimer, both

of whom belonged to the famous Frankfurt Institute for Social Research (Institut für Sozialforschung). As things turned out, those lectures did not prove very useful to me: Adorno was obscure; his lectures were fashionable gatherings of elegant girls and sophisticated members of the intelligentsia who flocked to listen to a philosopher most of them (I surmise) did not understand. Horkheimer was intellectually more accessible; he was also affable (he once asked me and a couple of German students to lunch, and I was greatly surprised by the fact that he had a chauffeur and took us to an expensive restaurant, a fact that to my naive and youthful mind was in strident contrast with his profession of modern and updated Marxism).

My wavering between strict methods of legal inquiry and recurrent forays into other disciplines came to the fore when, after graduation and on immediately becoming a research assistant, I tended to be a strict legalist in my supervision of LLM theses, repressing my own desires and tendencies. For example, this happened with one of my supervisees, Tiziano Terzani, who later became a famous reporter and writer on social and religious matters. A couple of years ago I met him again, after he had given a fascinating speech. Once the loud applause subsided, I told him how much I admired his narratory skills. He confided in a low voice that his decision to become a reporter and a writer was due to me. Faced with my astonishment, he reminded me that when in the summer of 1961 I had sent him back his thesis together with my comments, in order to sum up my criticisms of his flowery language and frequent meta-legal digressions, on the front page I had written, as a sort of warning, a phrase from Kant: 'Die Wissenschaft soll trocken sein' (science must be dry). This, he claimed, had prompted him to abandon all hopes of an academic legal career and to opt instead for journalism.

Torn between Positivism and Socially Oriented: Study of Law

ONE OF THE reasons for my doubts about the path to take was also linked to the legal method that at the time (and perhaps still now) prevailed in continental Europe: strict positivism. It is based on a rigid distinction between lex lata (the law in force) and lex ferenda (the law as it might be changed) and insists that lawyers should deal only with the former, and not with the question of whether law ought to be changed and how. In addition, lawyers should not meddle with social, historical, or sociological inquiries into the birth of lex lata. This approach, which concerned in particular the study of public law (private law, harking back to an old tradition, had remained immune from 'contamination' with other meta-legal disciplines), emerged in the late nineteenth century and was consolidated first in Germany and then in most European countries. In Italy it had been powerfully propounded by two distinguished publicists: Vittorio Emanuele Orlando (1860-1952) and Santi Romano (1875-1947), who both ended up as professors of public law at Rome University.

In the area of international law, one of the strongest advocates of the adoption of this method, a man whose stance tended to be more formal and positivist than that of Dionisio Anzilotti (1867-1950), was Tomaso Perassi (1886-1960), professor in Rome from 1928 to 1955. He was a highly respected and most influential scholar in Italy in his lifetime. I had the chance to meet him in his office at the Italian Constitutional Court, of which he was then vice-president. As a third year law student, I had written a detailed review of the latest edition of a masterly textbook of international law by the leading Austrian scholar Alfred Verdross (1890-1980).[1] My professor had carefully edited the review (I still have my typescript with his corrections) and then asked me personally to hand the revised text to Perassi, who also was the editor-in-chief of the leading Italian journal on international law (*Rivista di diritto internazionale*). Sperduti insisted that I should meet Perassi, who after all was my 'academic grandfather' (Sperduti being one of his disciples). I thus went to Rome full of trepidation to make the acquaintance of the great academic and judge. Unexpectedly, I found a very urbane old gentleman, who treated me, a young man of twenty, almost as a fellow scholar. He smiled with great benevolence, through two slits from which filtered a penetrating and – it seemed to me – sly glance, and did not say a word. Overwhelmed with awe and embarrassment, I talked and talked for about half an hour of my plans for the future, of Pisa University, of my predilection for international law, then, on seeing that he had not uttered a single word, I abruptly stopped, stood up, said goodbye and left. Only later, when I told one of Perassi's numerous senior disciples about my traumatic meeting with him did I learn that he was famous for being a man of few words; for instance, he would ask those who went to submit papers for publication to sit and read them aloud, after which he would say a couple of words either of rejection or of acceptance. Perassi was also the author of a remarkable booklet on legal methodology, where he concisely set out the fundamentals of the strictly positivist approach.[2] This approach led him to write papers on the Covenant of the League of Nations and – later – on the UN Charter that are notable for a dry and formalistic legal analysis that while superb in its delineation (marked by great legal rigor and exemplary lucidity) of the formal features of the two institutions, fails to explain the role and the significance of these institutions in the world community.[3] On reading these two essays, I was struck by how that legal method was incapable of delving beneath the legal surface of major political bodies of the international community. Those essays, as well as other writings by Perassi that appeared in the 1930s and 1940s, all perfectly technical and abstract, reminded me of a well-known poem by Fernando Pessoa (Ouivi contar que outrora, quando a Pérsia). The poem talks about two chess players in Persia who, unperturbed, carry on playing with great acumen and skill amidst the raging of an implacable war, their gaze fixed on the chessboard, bent only on thinking up the best move, while all around them houses are burning or are pillaged, women are being raped and children killed.[4]

Later on, however, I realized that this abstract positivist approach was important in at least two respects: it did away with the confusion between legal and historical or political inquiries, which had plagued many legal works in the nineteenth and early twentieth centuries; it enabled lawyers to keep politics at bay, thereby avoiding smuggling political or ideological leanings into scholarly inquiries. Still, this dry investigation of legal institutions – devoid of any consideration of their social context as well as hindering any move from the study of existing law to a proponent approach – did not satisfy me at all. I was later to discover the limitations of this approach when I read in the diaries of the Italian foreign minister Galeazzo Ciano some derogatory remarks about Perassi, who for many years during the fascist era had been first one of the legal advisers (from 1931-1936) and then the chief legal adviser to the Italian Foreign Ministry (between 1937-1943),[5] without however ever sharing the political views of fascist leaders or reflecting them in his legal writings, thanks to his positivism. Ciano noted on 9 April 1939 that he had to draft a document on the union between Italy and Albania (which, upon being attacked by Italian troops, had just capitulated); he then adds that he will have to consult with some 'professional pettifoggers' (professionisti del cavillo) at the Ministry (T. Perassi and two diplomats).[6] To my mind, this passage from Ciano's diaries confirmed the notion that, once he has embraced a strictly positivist approach, a lawyer may easily risk becoming a servant of the prince, although he can claim he is merely a 'technical expert'.

In the following years I also discovered another side of positivism: its role as a powerful shield of state sovereignty. Insistence on positivism played such a role, for instance, in Paris in 1919, when the two US members of the

'Commission on the Responsibility of the Authors of the War and on the Enforcement of the Penalties' set up at the Peace Conference strongly objected
to introducing the notion of 'offences against the laws of humanity' in future
trials against war criminals because 'the laws and principles of humanity are
not certain, varying with time, place and circumstances, and according, it
may be, to the conscience of the individual judge. There is no fixed and universal standard of humanity'.[7] It is striking that these considerations were
not reiterated in 1945 by the US delegation to the London Conference that
drafted the Charter of the International Military Tribunal at Nuremberg,
which included in Article 6 the notion of crimes against humanity, thereby
accepting that the laws of humanity were applicable in international law.
Similarly, by insisting on positivist considerations, the US, British and Italian members of the Advisory Committee of Jurists (appointed by the Council of the League of Nations in 1921 to draft the Statute of the Permanent
Court of International Justice) opposed a provision entrusting the future
Court with the task of applying 'principles of objective justice'. Indeed, as
the US member Root noted, 'nations will submit to positive law, but will not
submit to such principles as have not been developed into positive rules supported by an accord between all States'.[8] True, the 'principles of objective
justice' are undefined. But what is even more important is that the 'laws and
principles of humanity' were hazy in those days and could not be used as
criminal legal standards to prosecute individuals. Perhaps, however, if in
1919, compliance with the 'laws of humanity' had been proclaimed as a legal
imperative binding on all states, in 1939-45 the political and military leaders of some European States would have thought twice before trampling
upon the most elementary principles of human dignity. More generally, I
wonder whether one ought not to move beyond the strict legal parameters
agreed upon by States, at least whenever the need to oppose glaring injustice
would oblige one to do so. This concept, i.e. that one can exceptionally depart from positivism, was proclaimed in 1946 at Nuremberg by the International Military Tribunal, when it justified non-compliance with the nullum
crimen sine lege principle for the crime of aggression (as well as, implicitly,
for crimes against humanity). Indeed, the Tribunal not only stated that in
international law 'the maxim nullum crimen sine lege is not a limitation of
sovereignty, but is in general a principle of justice' (a proposition true at the
time, no longer valid today); but, more importantly, it also said, 'To assert
that it is unjust to punish those who in defiance of treaties and assurances
have attacked neighbouring states without warning is obviously untrue, for
in such circumstances the attacker must know that he is doing wrong, and

so far from it being unjust to punish him, it would be unjust if his wrong were allowed to go unpunished'.[9]

In any event, the two contradictory mindsets continued to coexist in me. A German friend from Frankfurt would scoff at my wavering between the two by quoting the well-known verses from Goethe about the two 'souls' living together in Faust, one of which wished to depart from the other.[10] I adopted a sort of scholarly 'Dr. Jekyll and Mr. Hyde' attitude. My first books and other writings were dry pieces of legal scholarship[11] of average value, I would say today. After getting a professorship and thus feeling freer to choose not only the subjects of my research but also the way to deal with them, I began to inquire into legal problems that had a strong human and social dimension: human rights and the humanitarian law of armed conflict. However, I tackled those problems from a strictly legal viewpoint, producing writings that perhaps might still be of interest – but only to scholars.

Nonetheless, I was not happy and kept grappling with the problem. I felt a lingering unease with traditional legal methods. A notion was haunting me. In a letter of 25 December 1896, an Italian philosopher, Antonio Labriola, who had eventually embraced socialism in politics and the method of 'historical materialism' in his scholarly inquiries, wittily attacked the younger Italian philosopher Benedetto Croce for his post-Hegelian idealist views. He pointed out that philosophical idealism made him think of a schoolteacher in Naples who explained Plato's ideas by saying to his pupils that they were like caciocavallo (a kind of gourd-shaped cheese that in southern Italy is kept hanging from the ceiling so that it matures better).[12] In my imagination, the legal rules and the abstract, in-a-vacuum inquiries made into them by my fellow professors of law turned into those hanging pieces of cheese.

Then in the 1980s I gradually began to write for a larger audience. I had received a big push in this new direction from a few friendly after-dinner conversations in Oxford, in 1980, with the celebrated historian Arnaldo Momigliano (1908-1987), then fellow at All Souls College, where I was spending a year as a visiting fellow. In long walks, where I would keenly listen to his words while carefully avoiding the puddles all around us, he introduced me to the books and ideas of Moses Finley (1912-1986), the great American historian of antiquity. Finley's ability to combine rigorous historical method with the capacity to expound the results of his research in plain language, highly attractive even to the layman, struck me as an exemplary way to tackle scholarly problems. I thus published a string of books on topical issues discussed with an eye to the layman.[13] I now feel that, in the end, they did not attract either legal experts (who disparaged them as being merely intended to popularize legal topics) nor the wider audience they were targeted at.

This fluctuation between two poles has not stopped, I fear, as is shown from the various editions of a book of mine on the law of the international community.[14]

What is the ideal way of harmonizing the two tendencies? I believe that a lawyer should be able to inquire into a legal institution, a cluster of legal issues or a legal provision both by applying a strict and rigorous legal method and by inquiring into why the institution, the cluster of issues or the provision has been formed the way it has; or in other words, what political, social or economic motivations have led to the present configuration. Furthermore, a lawyer should not shy away from suggesting how the institution, the issues or the rules might be improved better to take account of social needs. I am aware that, once it is so formulated, this scientific program appears to be an easy task. I do not know to what extent I have proved up to this challenge in my endeavours. I did try to embrace this approach in a revisitation of my old theme of self-determination, but feel now that I failed.[15]

From Contemplation to Action

THIS HAS NOT been the only contradiction in my thinking and intellectual leanings. I have also been constantly torn between research and action. There was, on the one side, the desire to undertake research work in a rarefied place, far from the hubbub of daily life: the ideal place is an old library, such as the Codrington library at Oxford, or even a modern one, such as the law library of the Columbia Law School in New York, but then only on Sundays or late in certain evenings, when there are fewer people about. There I am at ease and at peace with myself, particularly if I have to peruse old textbooks or dusty collections of diplomatic documents or judicial cases. Being a bookworm is comfortable. Life is complex and thorny; it is sometimes less painful to look upon it from afar. Many will remember Lucretius' image of the man safely resting on the beach while a devastating storm is raging at sea,[16] where sailors in a ship are desperate to find shelter; or Montaigne's rather less cowardly observation that one should always have a 'back shop' (une arrière-boutique) available, where one can take refuge from the wearing chores of the day[17]. For all its attractions and advantages, I have always felt dissatisfied with this mindset. After a while, reality proves irresistible. I have thus made many attempts to move from 'paper life' to real life. This of course I could do only in a narrow area close to my professional competence. Thus, I started off as a 'para-diplomat' attending various international meetings held by organizations such as the United Nations and the Council of Europe. There you come in touch with diplomats, judges, politicians, and international civil servants. Attending the works of such bodies (the UN Commission on Human Rights, as it then was, or the Sub-Commission on Minorities, or the Council of Europe bodies on human rights) as a delegate or a member is a useful way to understand the actual operation of international dealings. What proved more insightful, however, was the experience gained in other bodies.

First came the Diplomatic Conference on the updating of the 1949 Geneva Conventions (1974-1977, preceded by two sessions of a Conference of Experts, 1971-1972). There, acting as a member of the Italian Government delegation, I managed to see how international treaties are hammered out and how much time delegations sometimes spend on wordings that are seemingly harmless but in fact conceal conflicting state interests. Perhaps on one or two occasions I also made a tiny contribution to enhancing the humanitarian scope of the laws of warfare, of course within the limited confines possible for a delegation that was bound to stick to NATO coordination and directives.[18]

A second experience that proved even more instructive was that as a member and chairman of the Council of Europe Committee against Torture. These were four years of gruelling work, visiting police stations, prisons and other places of detention throughout Europe, and then drafting reports with recommendations. However, these were years where for the first time in my life I moved from a relatively leisurely activity (studying, discussing, writing and lecturing) to stark confrontation with harsh realities: inspecting places where human beings were being detained and frequently ill-treated. I also gradually realized how important it is to be uncompromising when facing a reluctant state official who intends to deny you access to a police station or to a cell, or refuses to disclose information. In many instances, having received information that some special detainees were being hidden in certain cells, I demanded to visit them. Whenever I was found wrong, I apologized to the authorities. In many other cases, however, I was not wrong, and duly reported our findings. At the expiry of the first four-year term I resigned: I was burnt out and needed to recover from seeing so much evil. I also recovered by writing a small book, a sort of memoir, which to my regret had a weaker impact than I had hoped.[19] One of the lessons I learned in my visits to prisons, police stations, psychiatric asylums, deten tion centers for foreigners, and other places where persons are deprived of their liberty is that inhumanity is inextricably intertwined with our humanity; it is indeed part of our humanity. It is something that a French writer, Romain Gary, had already noted in one of his novels.[20]

A third and even more challenging experience was that of international criminal judge. In 1993 the UN General Assembly elected me as a judge with the International Criminal Tribunal for the former Yugoslavia. Soon after we were sworn in, I was elected President. In a matter of a few days I became engrossed in that task, which among other things obliged me to learn a great deal about areas that hitherto I had neglected, chiefly criminal and comparative law. I worked very hard to get the new judicial body off the ground. I think I managed to turn an organ that, when it was first established, almost everybody considered doomed to failure into an effective and indeed vibrant judicial institution. Sitting in judgement on criminal cases proved very demanding. I think that nevertheless I made a quite innovative if controversial contribution to the development of its case law. These, however, were trying days. I still remember an evening in November 2005 in New York. I had just reported to the General Assembly on the problems besetting the Tribunal and our endeavours to surmount them. There was a dinner with various diplomats, most of whom were French-speaking (which led all the others to switch to that language, out of courtesy). One of them asked me whether I thought that the Tribunal could become the momentous institution I was hoping for. I said that we were at a crucial point, a real turning point, a moment that could be described as 'make or break' (Ça passe ou ça casse, I said). The Dutch Ambassador to the UN joined in saying that he was sure we would make it (Ça passe, ça passe, car vous vous appelez 'Passese'). I thought this was a witty reward for my dogged efforts. However, there again, after six years of working with unsparing energy, I had to give up, and reluctantly resigned, in order to stave off a breakdown. It later dawned on me that one of my numerous defects was that of plunging into action, without occasionally retiring into that comfortable 'back shop' extolled by Montaigne.

Finally, in visiting the Sudan and in particular Darfur as the chairman of the UN Commission of Inquiry on Darfur in 2004-2005, I was able to draw upon both my experience as an inspector and my time spent as a judge. Conducting an in-depth inquiry in a brief time span was again exacting physically and psychologically, but I feel it was worth going through that ordeal. In retrospect, I consider myself very fortunate for having made these forays into real life. They enabled me to escape the danger of the 'intellectual' who, as Albert Einstein once noted, 'has no direct contact with life in the raw, but encounters it in its easiest, synthetic form – upon the printed page.'[21]

Confronting Evil

IN MY FORAYS into real life, I have had many opportunities to meet not only unsavory characters but also some truly striking representatives of the dark side of human nature. I vividly remember their faces.

One was the face of the young, short Turkish police officer who had beaten up and then raped a Kurdish girl (I met her, by mere chance, the next day: she was lying in her bunk in a prison cell, as pale as death, and it was only at the insistence of her cell mate that in the end she recounted her ordeal, describing her tormentor so minutely that I could not fail to recognize him in the police officer with whom I had talked at length the day before. His appearance had struck me, for he was so nervous, agitated and aggressive; when we shook hands at the end of the long interview in the police station, his hands were moist with sweat).

Another was the face of the tall and elegant chief of police in Ankara, who would smile at most of our questions and blatantly lie about facts as well as persons in detention, or arrogantly dismiss any cautious criticism we might make.

Then there was the face of some of the defendants in the dock at The Hague: former military personnel, but also political leaders or simple civilians who, although accused of appalling deeds, brazenly denied everything even when confronted with compelling testimony, and never showed even a scintilla of repentance.

It is, however, easier to spot the traces of Evil in the faces of the victims: their suffering can less easily be erased or concealed than the wickedness of their persecutors. I saw much suffering on the faces of the hundreds of detainees I met and interviewed in European prisons over four years; I saw sadness and suffering on the face of the Kurdish girl I mentioned above; I saw indelible suffering in so many witnesses we heard in court (their testimony was often so heart-rending that occasionally even the coldest and emotionally hardened judge could not avoid being deeply moved).

It should come as no surprise that with all these encounters, even more than my scholarly or quasi-diplomatic dealing with human rights, I was constantly faced with the age-old question of how it is possible for a human being to behave so inhumanely towards another human being? Perhaps philosophers or psychologists have found an answer, if only a tentative one. I have not. It is an agonizing question. It is the foundation of This is a man by Primo Levi. And the main reason why that book is so troubling: it is not only a book on Auschwitz; it is essentially a book where on each page the author asks himself: how was it possible for human beings to behave that way? And he leaves us with this harrowing question.

A modern philosopher, Benedetto Croce, once wrote that if inhumanity were not part of us, we could not understand Oedipus Rex, Macbeth or Othello. This remark is not sufficient, however. I have found some sense of orientation in the reflections of Martin Buber in Good and Evil (a work that, albeit based on theological thinking and inspired by deep religiosity, can also persuade a secularist like me). In this work, Buber notes that man has two innate urges: a 'good' one and an 'evil' one. 'In the creation of man,' says Buber, 'the two urges are set in opposition to each other. The Creator gives them to man as his two servants which, however, can only accomplish their service in genuine collaboration. The "evil urge" is no less necessary than its companion, indeed even more necessary than it, for without it man would woo no woman and beget no children, build no house and engage in no economic activity, for it is true that "all travail and all skill in work is the rivalry of a man with his neighbor" (Ecclesiastes 4:4). Hence this urge is called "the yeast in the dough", the ferment placed in the soul by God, without which the human dough does not rise. [...] of the two, it is the evil urge which is fundamental.' Buber adds that, 'Man's task [...] is not to extirpate the evil urge, but to reunite it with the good'. More generally, he notes that, 'This important doctrine cannot be understood as long as good and evil are conceived, as they usually are, as two diametrically opposite forces or directions. Its meaning is not revealed to us until we recognize them as similar in nature; the "evil" urge as passion, that is, the power peculiar to man, without which he can neither beget nor bring forth, but which, left to itself, remains without direction and leads astray; and the "good" urge as pure direction, in other words, as an unconditional direction, that towards God. To unite the two urges implies: to equip the absolute potency of passion with the one direction that renders it capable of great love and of great service. Thus and not otherwise can man become whole'. [22]

These thoughts have shed some light on my personal experience with Evil. I do not know, however, how well-founded they are. And, at any rate, they cannot set to rest our disquiet about what daily occurs around us and also within us. What should perhaps help us to attenuate our pessimism (and its inner equivalent, depression) so as to allow us to continue in our daily exertions is the awareness that there are, however, so many persons who channel their aggressive drive towards socially useful action. Also knowing that generosity, compassion and care for others are so widespread helps immensely. Elie Wiesel recounts in *La Nuit* that, upon arrival in 1944 at Auschwitz-Birkenau, one of those hopeless and wretched inmates furtively approached him and whispered not to say to the s s who interrogated all the new 'arrivals' that he was 15 and his father 50 ('tell them that you are 18 and your father 40').[23] That unknown detainee, moved only by genuine compassion, thus saved them from immediate gasification.

Major Areas of Scholarly Interest

IF I NOW take a look at the subjects in which I have been interested and on which I have toiled so hard in my scholarly activity, it appears to me that they boil down to a very few areas, and always the same ones: human rights, the self-determination of peoples, the humanitarian laws regulating armed conflicts, the use of force by states, and more generally legal restraints on violence in the world community; and international criminal law. Probably it was the desire to understand both what motivates states to use violence and what we individuals can do to mitigate violence that prompted me to explore these areas of international law. These are areas where the relation between force and legal standards aiming at restraining force is more problematic; areas where the legal network thins and is full of holes, and therefore the observer may better grasp the power relations that exist between the primary actors on the international scene: the sovereign states. Not unwittingly, I was moved by the old maxim of Roman wisdom: hominum causa omne jus constitutum est (any rule of law is ultimately made on account of human beings). This maxim had been instilled in me by the teachings of my professor at Pisa, Giuseppe Sperduti (1912-1993). He was a profound and acute scholar, whose writings were unfortunately marred by obscurity and an overindulgence in logical or theoretical musings. Also, like most lawyers of his generation of the 1930s and 1940s in Germany and Italy, he was obsessed with originality: he was always quick to stress that he had been the first to propound certain views. More generally, he was constantly asking himself who had been the first to say what, as if views and ideas were physical objects that one possesses and hence can lend or sell but of which one may always claim ownership, and not unstable and evanescent phantasms, often generated in many persons' minds and soon to be found in general circulation. He started off as a positivist academic politically close to fascism, then, in the aftermath of the Second World War, he gradually rediscovered his Catholic ideological origins and became increasingly attracted to human rights. He ended up a staunch and indeed formidable supporter of human rights, far from the state idolatry of his early positivism. As a member of the European Commission of Human Rights for many years (1960-1992), he played an important role in pushing through an expansive interpretation of many provisions of the European Convention on Human Rights. It was he who insisted so much on the need for international law to be oriented towards human beings.[24] When working as a judge at The Hague, I managed to have that Latin maxim I cited above accepted by my fellow judges. I put it into a judgment on which I had spent much labor, Tadic (Interlocutory appeal).[25]

I still believe that only those problems that dramatically affect the daily life of human beings are worth studying. I still believe that it is the cluster of legal rules and institutions that may have a dramatic impact on the life and suffering of human beings that should constitute the main focus of our attention as scholars.

A Decisive Encounter

ONE OF THE advantages of my profession has been the chance to meet so many notable persons: scholars, diplomats, judges, and military experts. In my private life I have also had the fortune to meet various writers and philosophers, some of whom I have come to know fairly well. I have always endeavored to distil as much as possible from these encounters, in terms of knowledge, human experience and vision. I unconsciously heeded the repeated advice of my parents (advice that harked back to the fundamental wisdom of the oral cultural tradition of poor areas): 'always seek the company of those who are better than you and also pay for their expenses'.

Of these many encounters, the one that had the greatest influence on me was that with B.Y.A. Röling. He was a Dutch criminal lawyer who, when still fairly young, had been a judge in the Tokyo trial of the major Japanese war criminals in 1946-47. Then, back in his own country, he had turned to international law. I first met him in Strasbourg in 1973, when he, Pierre Boissier (a Swiss expert in humanitarian law), and I had been invited to give lectures on the laws of warfare. Röling and I became friends and frequently met until his death in 1985. He was impressive: tall, with sharp blue eyes, snow-white hair and, what impressed me most, a soft yet deeply persuasive voice. He would never raise his voice, never get angry. What struck the listener was his enormous human experience coupled with his command of various fields of knowledge (law, peace research, history, political science, sociology). In 1958 he had fallen out with the Dutch Ministry of Foreign Affairs (which had until then sent him as a Dutch delegate to the UN General Assembly) because in December 1957, on his journey back from New York, taking advantage of the leisure time offered by the ship, he had written a little book in which he stressed the urgent need for the Netherlands to grant independence to Irian (Western Guinea), then a Dutch colony.[26] He was immediately struck off the list of Dutch delegates to the UN. He never complained about this personal setback. Similarly, he never complained about not being appointed professor at the most prestigious Dutch University, that of Leiden, because of his unorthodox stance. It is only from some of his disciples that I later learned of these personal disappointments. Unlike most of us, he succeeded in reconciling himself with academic life, and never bore a grudge.

Röling was not a profound scholar; nor did he ever write one of those magnificent books where you feel that the author, in addition to opening new vistas, offers a refined and fully elaborated text. His major and most enduring scholarly work is a booklet he wrote in 1960: *International Law in an Expanded World*. A work that was not notable for the rigor of the argumentation or the elegance of the exposition, but a powerful book that departed from traditional legal scholarship, and by drawing upon history, sociology and international relations, it had two great merits: first, it presented an extremely original and challenging view of the history of the international community, its composition and its tensions; second, it took a 'progressive' stance, siding with what he used to call the 'underdogs', the 'have-nots', in short, the developing countries, and calling to action all those who, tired of a Eurocentric or Western-centric outlook, were bent on changing international relations. This was not at all a traditional, 'objective' law book; it was a 'livre de bataille' that shrewdly used and amalgamated various disciplines to take a fresh and insightful look at international relations. It was a book that stood squarely on the side of the underprivileged.

Röling taught me a lot. He had a fascinating capacity to talk about the many episodes culled from his vast experience. I remember that once, at a conference, he gently but firmly attacked me. I had presented a paper on the prohibition of weapons causing unnecessary suffering. Having investigated state practice in depth, I had concluded that prohibition was pointless, for states had never complied with it. Thus, I said, the prohibition was to be held devoid of any legal force. He took the floor and fiercely dissented. He noted that international principles may serve as legal standards even when they are unheeded, be it for a short time or for a much longer time. And he stressed that if a scholar adds his own scepticism to the inherent fragility of legal tenets restraining the use of violence, eventually if unwittingly he plays a negative role, helping to hamstring the reign of law. International principles, he added, may lie dormant for a time; but they are there, and sooner or later they may be used by one or more international actors to curb violence.

The Evolution of the International Community

I HAVE NOW come to a point in life where I ought to prepare for the return to darkness. It is a time for pause and reflection.

I may thus perhaps venture some general reflections on the international community and say how I appraise both the developments that have occurred in that community in my lifetime and the general outlook for the legal standards governing international dealings.

In my lifetime I have witnessed the evolution of three stages of the world community: when it was a community militarily and politically divided into two blocs split into western, socialist, and developing countries (1950-1989); when with the collapse of the Soviet bloc, it became a community dominated by one superpower, which however was not mighty enough to rule over all of the community and had to compromise on many issues with other major powers (1990-2000); and when the community, whilst remaining structured as before, has been overwhelmed by the threat of terrorism, so much so that most dealings of the major international actors are now influenced by the question of how to stem or destroy terrorism (2001 to the present). This is a period that some have termed the Fourth World War (the third being the Cold War).

In the first of these three stages, the military and political authority of the Soviet bloc was underpinned by a strong ideology that also permeated those states' attitude towards the international community. The fundamental principles advocated by that group of states were: protection of each state's sovereignty; the fight against western economic penetration and colonialism; and ideological, political and military expansion in other areas of the world. Everything was subordinated to those tenets. Even the self-determination of peoples was proclaimed only as a device for disrupting colonialism, racial segregation of the majority by a white minority (apartheid), as well as, after 1967, as a means of restraining Israel's occupation of the West

Bank and the Gaza Strip. Self-determination understood as the free and un-hindered choice by the people of their rulers through a multi-party system reflecting the various groupings in society was anathema to them. Similarly, human rights were only proclaimed to attack the West. International scrutiny of the way in which human rights were implemented in those states was out of the question. Nevertheless, it was thanks to this strong anti-Western position on the part of socialist states that developing countries were able to set forth their own ideology based on the same tenets plus an emphasis on economic development, and therefore to propound a restructuring of international economic relations. All this was accompanied, in developing countries, by a naive belief in the magical power of words and of the force of resolutions adopted by the UN General Assembly. Western states essentially remained on the defensive, clinging to traditional principles and trying to maintain the existing order as much as possible, even though the unraveling of colonialism was ineluctable. Their legal experts, however, were manifestly more sophisticated and argued their points with a better logic than those representing the other two groupings. Whatever the merits of each of the three blocs, it is a fact that international legal standards could only emerge if they mustered a large measure of support in all three. Hence, when drawing up new legal rules, an effort to understand and accept the viewpoint of other groups was always necessary. This process rendered negotiations on international legal standards difficult from a practical viewpoint, but it also made them intellectually fascinating. The drafting, between 1962 and 1970, and the adoption, in 1970, of the famous 'Declaration on Friendly Relations' (General Assembly resolution 2625-XXV, of 24 October 1970) was the culmination of this long process.

Owing to the clash of opposing ideologies, this was the period when new concepts were formulated and introduced into the legal network regulating the world community. Chief among them were the notions of obligations erga omnes and of jus cogens, as well as the duty of cooperation. They were generous attempts to accomplish two major objectives. First, to insert new values, endowed with universal force and binding on all people regardless of their conduct, within a legal structure traditionally based on self-interest, of the formal equality of all members and strict reciprocity of obligations. Second, to establish a hierarchy of values, where the new values must be overriding and all-embracing.

The downfall of socialism among other things entailed not only the disappearance of a strong front of socialist states but also the gradual demise of the ideological arsenal that developing countries had been using. Today this group substantially concentrates on economic claims linked to its underdevelopment. These states no longer propound principles or standards that in some way underpin or buttress a general outlook. The ideological absence of these states has divided the world community into two camps, lined up no longer along political or ideological principles, but rather along considerations of economic and military power. International legal discourse has thus become relatively less variegated than before. Probably the only major achievement of this period is the astounding success of the ideal of international criminal justice, which has led to a proliferation of international criminal courts and tribunals. Another sign of progress can perhaps be seen in the expanding force of the doctrine of human rights, which is no longer marred by ideological manipulation and abuse. As a result, the only weapon still in the hands of the, alas, numerous authoritarian states is the doctrine of domestic jurisdiction, which has consequently gone through a revival (particularly at the hands of China).

After September 2001 the social structure of the world community remained substantially unchanged, subject to two exceptions. First, new actors have emerged and asserted their presence with the greatest vigor: notably, non-state militarily organized groups, mostly with terrorist leanings. Secondly, some developing states (China, India, Pakistan, Brazil, South Africa) have become major powers, and some of them are also endowed with nuclear weapons. What has dramatically changed, however, is the political philosophy embraced by states. There is now a huge divide between states and non-state organizations espousing a terrorist outlook and states threatened by and hence opposed to terrorism. In sum, terrorism and its philosophy have become the major divide in the world community. The new aspect is that terrorism is also increasingly associated with Islam, all the more so because one of the favorite and most lethal methods of terrorist combat is self-sacrifice (suicide bombers).

At present, the world community is thus split into two camps: in one there are persons, organizations and states bent on destroying Western civilization by any means, no matter how cruel they have to be and no matter who the victims might be; the other camp is under the sway of those only eager to fight back by dint of the overwhelming force of weapons. There is no dialogue and no attempt in either camp to understand the motivations and aspirations of the adversary. Armed conflicts have thus spread at a staggering pace; sometimes no distinction can be made between international and internal armed conflicts, as mixed conflicts are becoming more and more frequent and, even more dramatically, more asymmetrical. By the same token, the body of law designed to regulate and restrain armed violence, that is, international humanitarian law, has acquired enormous importance; however, as I will note below, at the same time its basic failings have conspicuously come to light. On top of that, we are still faced with a striking contradiction: the Five Permanent Members of the Security Council, who make up the 'board of directors' of the international community[27] and under the UN Charter should be responsible for ensuring peace and stability, are the biggest manufacturers and exporters of weapons, which they primarily export to developing countries.

The Hallmarks of the Present World Community

IF I TAKE a look at the legal standards and the legal institutions of the world community as they have evolved in the last twenty or thirty years, I cannot help feeling dispirited. The great promises heralded in the 1960s and 1970s – the upholding of forward-looking notions such as obligations erga omnes, 'obligations owed to the international community as a whole',[28] jus cogens, the aggravated responsibility of states, the common heritage of mankind, the right to development – have remained unfulfilled. Thirty or forty years later, these notions have still not been acted upon by states or judicial organs. They still do not have the strength to guide the day-to-day activities of the primary actors on the world stage. Furthermore, the body of law designed to restrain states from resorting to military force has remained full of loopholes: neither the doctrine of anticipatory self-defence nor that of resort to force on humanitarian grounds has been clarified by states or the United Nations. The two major flaws of international humanitarian law have not been remedied, namely: the failure to restrain the conduct of hostilities through the enactment of detailed and precise legal standards designed to protect civilians more effectively, and the failure to ensure impartial and constant monitoring of breaches of the law on the part of the combatants. Human rights law, the most significant hallmark of the new international community reborn in the aftermath of the Second World War, has not made much headway. The gap between standard-setting and implementation remains conspicuous. The replacement of the UN Human Rights Commission with the Human Rights Council has not involved any major change: that body still remains in the hands of sovereign states, bent on playing politics more than ensuring respect for human dignity. The law of the sea has been stripped of its most progressive concept, that of 'com mon heritage of mankind', thus returning to traditional notions based on reciprocity and joint interests. The law and institutions of development, of trade, in particular the WTO, as well as the law of the environment are plodding along, strained by the effort to keep up with the mushrooming of the often intractable problems of poverty, underdevelopment, large-scale pollution, and global warming.

In addition, some concepts generously propounded in the aftermath of the Second World War, in particular that of the self-determination of peoples, have failed to be realized. It is a sad fact that neither in Palestine (since 1967 at least) nor in Western Sahara (since 1975 or at least 1991) has this concept proved efficacious as a tool for liberating those peoples. True, the problems are exceedingly complex, and the political and military implications of any solution stand in the way of a rapid settlement. The problems are left to fester, however, and states do not see any incentive in a principle that instead should serve as one of their major guiding lights.

In short, the traditional 'soul' of the world community has continued to march on unperturbed. Only its surface has been lightly scratched by those new values and legal standards. The world community continues to be dominated by sovereign states, each of which is primarily bent on the pursuit of its own short- or medium-term interests.

On top of that, fundamentalist ideologies are pervading the world: some in favor of violent subversion and terror, others – admittedly not dangerous, albeit very worrisome – in favor of the exportation of Western democracy to the whole world, if need be by force of arms. These ideologies, whatever their implications, are a far cry from the ideals enshrined in the UN Charter: peace, respect for human rights (that is, toleration and understanding) and the self-determination of peoples (that is, the freedom of peoples from the oppression of foreign countries).

What compounds this rather gloomy picture is the dearth of great leaders capable of taking to heart and putting their minds at the service of the world community. The only great living visionary, Nelson Mandela, has retired on age and health grounds. There is no Franklin Delano Roosevelt, Churchill, or de Gaulle around. In his *Philosophy of History* (1823-31) Hegel defined this category of persons Welt-Historische Individuen, world-historical individuals, 'soul leaders' (Seelenführer), 'men who [have] an insight into the requirements of the time of what [is] ripe for development', men who 'will and do accomplish something great'.[29] If one of those men were with us, he could perhaps inject new ideas into the fabric of the world community and push through solutions to some of the festering problems currently polluting that community: for instance, the Palestinian question, the problem of Western Sahara, the numerous armed conflicts with all the attendant atrocities in Africa, the plight of the populations in many developing countries that find it hard to build modern and democratic state structures, or the question of global warming.

As a consequence, there seems to be no more room for innovative concepts such as those that emerged in the first of the various stages of development of the world community. Except for international criminal justice and the vigorous life of regional judicial bodies protecting human rights (in Europe and Latin America), there is a dearth of international actors pursuing ideals and concerns not subordinated to self-interest.

In sum, the world community is still bedeviled by the huge gap between generous and visionary legal rhetoric and the harsh reality of states each substantially pursuing its own national interests. The generous promises and projects made in the 1960s and 1970s have not materialized. It is as if states, after much discussion and interminable polemics on its placement and configuration, had built a magnificent skyscraper, provided it with an entrance, floors, stairs, lifts, fully furnished rooms, and even vases full of freshly cut flowers, and then left the building empty, for nobody dares to enter and live there.

The outlook is grim. The lawyer, faced with what seems a partial eclipse of reason, more and more often feels like a person painting 'still lifes' on the walls of a sinking ship.

Does an International Community Proper Exist?

THE CRUCIAL ISSUE is whether an international community proper exists. No doubt it does exist as a myth, and this myth was explored in a masterly way by Rene Jean Dupuy.[30] But does it also exist as a living reality? The question was raised in lucid terms in 1936 by a leading British scholar, James Brierly.[31] His answer, written in dark times when a world war and its attendant devastation were looming large, was very nuanced.

Today, some of the trappings of a community proper are visible. There are legal standards regulating the conduct of all the members of the community, whatever their size, status, development, and military and economic power. There are legal institutions embracing all the states: the United Nations and the UN family of specialized agencies. There is a sort of constitution, the UN Charter, which sets out the goals that international institutions ought to pursue and also lays down the general principles by which states should abide: peace, friendly relations, interstate co-operation, respect for human rights, the self-determination of peoples. There also exist legal standards that restrain the previously absolute liberty of states to regulate their own actions and dealings: these are the peremptory norms to which I referred a moment ago, the so-called jus cogens.

What however is lacking is a 'community sentiment', the feeling in each member state that it is a part of the whole and must pursue common goals; a shared conviction that each member not only must comply with existing legal and moral standards, but is also bound to call upon and even demand that other members do likewise in the interest of the whole community. In each national system there exist both strong bonds within the community and also public institutions that in a way cement or replace those bonds. True, all too often in modern cities passers-by look the other way when they see a person lying wounded on a street or otherwise in need of aid. But then, public institutions (police officers, hospital officials, and so on) or private organizations (charities, and other non-profit bodies) step in to provide relief; their action is a surrogate for the sense of humanity lacking in single individuals. In the world community, members are instead still self-oriented, and adequate public institutions are lacking. True, there are public bodies that should incarnate this community sentiment and speak out on behalf of the whole community when one or more members grossly deviate from accepted standards in matters that should be of major concern for everyone. But they are either silent or timid, or their voice is not loud enough. Ethiopia and Eritrea, two very poor countries that need to promote economic development and education and eradicate widespread poverty, were engaged instead in an all-out war (1998-2000). Other states have done very little to stop this aberration. The fundamental human rights of their own citizens are violated by governments on a daily basis in dozens of countries: from Myanmar (Burma) to China, to the Democratic Republic of Congo, to the Sudan, and to many former Soviet republics. Third states look on and make appeals at best. Some UN bodies adopt resolutions or send 'rapporteurs' to draw up reports to which very few pay attention. When the United States touted the existence of a third category between lawful combatants and civilians, that of 'unlawful combatants' (deprived of the rights and immunities of civilians as well as the immunity from prosecution for legitimate acts of war, which accrues to belligerents), one would have expected that the ICRC, as the guardian of international humanitarian law, as well as other states would vigorously reject this category as contrary to existing law. Nothing happened. The ICRC visited Guantanamo, producing confidential reports on the treatment of unlawful combatants there, and issued general statements on the various categories of persons involved in armed hostilities. Similarly, when the United States engaged in ill-treating detainees in Iraq, no state protested or demanded respect for international standards against torture and inhumane and degrading treatment. The UN Committee against Torture passed a report calling upon the US to abide by the 1984 Convention on Torture. Is that enough? Similarly, no firm protest accompanied by a demand for the cessation of its repeated breaches of law has been made to Russia for its action in Chechnya. Only the European Court of Human Rights has on a few occasions found Russia in breach of the European Convention. Furthermore, the international community, through the United Nations, has consistently expressed its concern over the situation in Darfur, the civil war raging in the Democratic Republic of Congo and other African states, as well as the intolerable breaches of human rights in Zimbabwe and Myanmar (Burma). However, the gap between the action taken and the suffering – as well as the needs – of the population there is enormous: the plight of the individuals in those countries wholly dwarfs international action.

In short: can we consider that these faint voices express the community sentiment I was evoking above?

The Outlook for the World Community

THE 'COSMOPOLITAN SOCIETY' dreamed of by Kant, a federation of free states that absolutely ban war and live in a condition of 'good neighbourliness', is still far off. The world community is destined to remain dominated by self-interested and therefore permanently clashing sovereign states for many years. The 'evil nature of man, which can be observed clearly in the free relations between nations', to take up Kant's words,[32] will continue to plague the world community for a long time.

The idea of a world government must a fortiori be ruled out, unless a natural catastrophe of immense proportions or a new world conflagration resulting from an increase in friction between the Great Powers brings about such a change that a reborn world community is transformed into a world state.

The more plausible prospect is that of a gradual strengthening of regional bonds. In twenty or thirty years this development could lead to the formation of regional organized groups centrally running regional affairs and ensuring relative peace within each group. Judicial or executive regional agencies could be set up to ensure that shared values are applied within each group. Such groups might also establish enforcement agencies capable not only of looking after regional concerns but also of acting on behalf of the world community (say, in contact with and upon the authorization of the UN Security Council) to impose peace, law and order in other areas of the world by the use of force.

Thus, although an international community proper would not yet exist, at least some building blocks would be put in place for the eventual restructuring of society and a better distribution of power.

Let Us Heed Our Daimon

WITH HINDSIGHT, I feel that while perhaps my 'practical' action has been somehow helpful, I have not contributed much to legal scholarship. However, from the outset I have been sceptical about writing books. One writes a book with ardour and hope and tries to inject into it as many new ideas and views and scholarship as possible; while one is writing a book, everything else wanes in importance, as if that book were the linchpin of the world. I have never forgotten, however, some thoughts by Arthur Schopenhauer I read many years ago. He wrote that, according to Herodotus, Xerxes wept at the sight of his enormous army, made up of so many lusty and valiant warriors, thinking that, of all these men, none would be alive in a hundred years' time. 'So,' added the philosopher, 'who cannot but weep at the sight of the thick fair catalogue to think that, of all these books, not one will be alive in ten year's time.'[33] I am afraid that most of our books have an even shorter life span. This, however, is not grounds for weeping. There are other, more serious grounds.

Philosophers teach us that, whatever the general circumstances of life, one ought to heed one's own daimon and accomplish the task of the day, however modest and tiny one's performance may be. It would be pusillanimous to stop striving for something higher than our day-to-day, life-sustaining job, only because the times are very gloomy indeed. Let us therefore march on and engage in our daily exertions – whatever their value – on the socio-legal problems that affect human beings. The hope that we may be able to pass on something intellectually and emotionally valuable to our children and grandchildren is an abiding solace. An academic also has another great joy: the hope that he or she has taught a way of thinking to a goodly number of young persons. I am overjoyed to see that some of those to whom I have tried to teach the use of the intellectual tools of our job are now faring so well and have surpassed me by far in the quality of their thinking.

When the ineluctable hour comes, it will find us neither dismayed nor slothful.

Notes

....

*   *Soliloquy* appeared in The Human Dimension of International Law. Selected Papers. Oxford University Press 2008.

1   The book was A. Verdross, *Völkerrecht*, 3rd edn (Wien: Springer Verlag, 1955). The review was published in 40 *Rivista di diritto internazionale*, 1957, 653-6.

2   *Introduzione alle scienze giuridiche* (Rome: ed Forato italiano, 1938), reprinted in T. Perassi, *Scritti giuridici*, I (Milan: Giuffrè, 1858), 3-52.

3   'L'ordinamento della Società delle Nazioni' in *La vita italiana*, 1920, 411-29, reprinted in *Scritti giuridici*, cit., 307-325; *L'ordinamento delle Nazioni Unite* (Padova: Cedam, 1950), reprinted in *Scritti giuridici* cit., 339-85.

4   This also applies to those papers by the eminent international lawyer, devoted to topical issues, always dissected in a dry and legalistic manner. See for instance the essay on the Spanish constitution of 1931, where the great novelties of that Constitution are either missing or not discussed ('La nuova Costituzione spagnola ed il diritto internazionale', in *Rivista di diritto internazionale* (1932), 453-6, reprinted in *Scritti giuridici*, cit., I, 411-14). However, most of his writings that appeared in those years were instead devoted to technical issues. See for instance 'Le assicurazioni sociali nel diritto internazionale' (1931) in *Scritti II*, 129-50; 'Consoli ed agenti diplomatici; Immunita in material penale'(1932), *ibid.*, 3-5; 'Su l'esenzione degli agenti diplomatici dalla giudsdizione' (1932), *ibid.*, 9-13; 'I caratteri formali della clausola facoltative sulla giurisdizione obbligatoria della Corte Permanente di Giustizia internazionale' (1932), *ibid.*, 25-30; 'Sull'articolo 22 del trattato del Laterano' (1937), *ibid.*, 453-4. Numerous other papers dealt with issues of private international law.

5   G. Morelli ('Tomaso Perassi', in 45 *Rivista di diritto internazionale* (1962), 3-14) hints at this activity (at 5). Detailed information is provided by F. Salerno (La *Rivista* e gli studi di diritto internazionale nel periodo 1906-1943, in 90 *Rivista di diritto internazionale* (2007), at 310, note 22). No mention is made by C. Mortati ('L'opera di Tomaso Perassi', in 45 *Rivista di diritto internazionale* (1962), 204-16).

6   G. Ciano, *Diario*, vol. I (1939-1940), 6th edn (Milan: Rizzoli, 1950), at 78. The two diplomats were Gino Buti (1888-1972), later ambassador to the Vichy Govern

ment, and Leonardo Vitetti (1895-1973), Director-General of General Affairs at the Foreign Ministry.

7   See 'Report Presented to the Preliminary Peace Conference by the Mission on the Responsibility of the Authors of War and on the Enforcement of Penalties', namely: *Violations of the Laws and Customs of War, Report of Majority and Dissenting Reports of American and Japanese Members of the Commission of Responsibilities, Conference of Paris* 1919 (Oxford: Clarendon Press, 1919), at 73.

8   League of Nations, PCI, Advisory Committee of Jurists, *Proces-verbaux of the Proceedings of the Committee* (The Hague: Van Langenhuysen Brothers, 1920), at 287.

9   *Trial of the Major War Criminals Before the International Military Tribunal – Nuremberg 14 November 1945-1 October 1946* (Nuremberg: International Military Tribunal, 1947), at 219 (emphasis added).

10 *Zwei Seelen wohnen, ach! in meiner Brust, Die eine will sich von der andern trennen; Die eine halt, in derber Liebeslust, Sich an die Welt mit klammernden Organen; Die andere hebt gewaltsam sich vom Dust Zu den Gefilden hoher Ahnen.* (Faust I, 1112-1117).

11 *Il diritto interno davanti al giudice internazionale* (Padua: Cedam, 1962); *Il controllo internazionale* (Milan: Giuffre, 1972).

12 Extracts from the letter are cited by B. Croce in his essay 'Come nacque e come morì il marxismo teorico in Italia (1895-1900): da lettere e ricordi personali', published as an annex in A. Labriola, *La concezione materialistica della storia*, 2nd edn (Bari: Laterza, 1946), 265-312, at 296 (this is what Labriola wrote: 'A proposito. Sai come un professore di Liceo del Salvatore (prima del '60) – prete di mestiere e frequentatore del botteghino del Carpo di Napoli, dove dava ai passanti i numeri del lotto definiva le idee di Platone agli scolari: *Figurateve tante casecavalle appise.*').

13 *Violence and Law in the Modern Age* (Oxford: Polity Press, 1988); Terrorism, Politics and Law – The Achille Lauro Affair (Oxford: Polity Press, 1989); Human Rights in a Changing World (Oxford: Polity Press, 1990); B.Y.A. Röling, *The Tokyo Trial and Beyond – Reflections of a Peacemonger* (edited by A. Cassese) (Oxford: Polity Press, 1993); Inhuman States – Imprisonment, Detention and Torture in Europe Today (Oxford: Polity Press, 1996).

14 See *International Law in a Divided World* (Oxford: Clarendon Press, 1986); *International Law* (Oxford: Oxford University Press, 2001); see also the 2nd edn (*ibid.*, 2005).

15 *Self-determination of Peoples – A Legal Reappraisal* (Cambridge: Cambridge University Press, 1995).

16 *Lucretius, De Rerum Natura,1, 1-6 'Suave, mari magno turbantibus aequora ventis, le terra magnum alterius spectare laborem/non quia vexari quemquamst iucunda voluptas,/sed quibus ipse malis careas quia cemere suave est/Suave etiam belli certamina magna tueri/per campos instructa tua sine parte pericli'.* ('What joy it is, when out at sea the

storm winds are lashing the waters, to gaze from the shore at the heavy stress some other man is enduring! Not that anyone's afflictions are in themselves a source of delight; but to realize from what troubles you yourself are free is joy indeed. What joy, again, to watch opposing hosts marshaled on the field of battle when you have yourself no part in their peril!', Lucretius, *On the Nature of the Universe*, trans. R.E. Latham (Penguin Books, 1979) at 60).

17   Montaigne, *Les Essais* (1595), I, xxxviii *'Il se faut réserver une arrière-boutique, toute nôtre, toute franche [i.c. libre], en laquelle nous établissons notre vraie liberté et principale retraite et solitude. En cette-ci faut-il prendre notre ordinaire entretien, de nous a nous-mêmes, et si privé, que nulle accointance au communication de chose étrangere y trouve place.'* Michel Seigneur de Montaigne, *Les Essais* (ed 1595) (Librairie Generale Franaise, 2001) at 372-3.

18   As a result of my participation in and observation of the Geneva Diplomatic Conference, I wrote two papers that perhaps are still worth some attention: 'The Prohibition of Indiscriminate Means of Warfare', in R.J. Akkerman, P.J. van Krieken, C.O. Pannenborg (eds), *Declarations on Principles – A Quest for International Peace* (Leyden: Sijthoff. 1977), 171-94; *'Means of Warfare: the Traditional and the New Law'*, in A. Cassese (ed.), *The New Humanitarian Law of Armed Conflict* (Napoli: Editoriale Scientifica, 1979), 162-98. I also wrote 'A Tentative Appraisal of the Old and the New Humanitarian Law of Armed Conflict (*ibid.*, 461-501), *'Mercenaries: Lawful Combatants or War Criminals?'*, in *Zeitschrift für ausländisches öffentliches Recht* (1980) 1ff; 'The Status of Rebels Under the 1977 Geneva Protocol on Non-International Armed Conflict', *International and Comparative Law Quarterly* (1981) 416ff; *'Wars of National Liberation and Humanitarian Law'*, in C. Swinarski (ed.), *Etudes et essais en l'honneur de J. Pictet* (Geneva-The Hague, M Nijholf, 1984), 313ff.

19   *Inhuman States – Imprisonment, Detention and Torture in Europe Today* (Oxford: Polity Press, 1996).

20   In his novel *Les Cerf-volants* (Paris: Gallimard, 1980) after stressing that what was terrible about Nazism was its 'inhuman side', he added that 'il faut bien se rendre à l'évidence: ce côté inhumain fait partie de l'humain. Tant qu'on ne reconnaîtra que l'inhumanité est chose humaine, on restera dans le mensonge pieux' (at 265).

21   A. Einstein, in A. Einstein and S. Freud, *Why war?* (Paris: International Institute of International Cooperation-League of Nations, 1933), at 19.

22   M. Buber, *Good and Evil – Two Interpretations* (Upper Saddle River, NJ: Prentice Hall, n.d.), at 94, 95, and 97.

23   E. Wiesel, *La Nuit* (1958) (Paris: Les Editions de Minuit, 2007), at 72.

24   I tried to outline the major contribution made by Giuseppe Sperduti to international law in a paper written after his death ('Note sull'opera di Giuseppe Sperduti', in 77 *Rivista di diritto internazionale* (1994), 313-25). There I stressed that to

'commemorate' Sperduti would mean to do him a disservice: he was a man with a strong critical mind, always eager to critically appraise ideas, views and persons. To write about him without assessing his scientific merits but also his scholarly weaknesses would mean to betray his intellectual and moral legacy.

25   ICTY, Appeals Chamber, *Decision on the Defence Motions for Interlocutory Appeal on Jurisdiction*, 2 October 1995 (case no IT-94-I-AR72), § 97.

26   B.V.A. Röling, *New Guinea als Wereldprobleem* (Assen: Van Gorcum and Co., 1958). After critically outlining the debates on New Guinea (Irian) in the UN General Assembly (at 45-78), Röling put forward his own views about the need for the Netherlands to relinquish its authority over the colony, setting forth two alternatives: either the colony was to be handed over to Indonesia, or the Netherlands was to entrust the UN with the task of deciding on the matter (at 79-104).

27   H. Kissinger, *Diplomacy* (New York-London: Simon and Schuster, 1995) spoke first of President F.D. Roosevelt envisioning 'a postwar order in which the three victors, along with China, would act as a board of directors of the world' (at 395).

28   Now proposed in Article 42 of the International Law Commission's Articles on State Responsibility.

29   G.W.F. Hegel, *Vorlesungen über die Philosophie der Weltgeschichte* (text of 1840 edn by G. Lasson, 2nd edn, Hamburg: F. Meinert, 1920, at 77-8).

30   See in particular *Communauté internationale et disparités de développement*, in 165 *Hague Recueil*, 1979-IV, 9-232; *La communauté internationale entre le mythe et l'histoire* (Paris: Economica, 1986). The same topic is also discussed in *L'Humanité dans l'imaginaire des nations* (Paris: Julliard, 1991), but in philosophical and literary terms.

31   'The Rule of Law in International Society' (1936), reprinted in J.L. Brierly, *The Basis of Obligation in International Law and Other Papers*, selected and edited by H. Lauterpacht and C.H.M. Waldock (Oxford: Clarendon Press, 1958), 250-64.

32   *Eternal Peace* (1795), in I. Kant, *Moral and Political Writings*, ed. by C.J. Friedrich (New York: The Modern Library, 1977), at 442.

33   A. Schopenhauer, *Essays and Aphorisms*, edited by R.J. Hollingdale (Penguin Books, 1970), at 209.

Reflections on the Current Prospects of International Criminal Justice*

ANTONIO CASSESE

Introduction
....

THE INCREASING IMPORTANCE of international criminal justice is no doubt a welcome development of the present international community. This importance is testified by both the proliferation of *international* criminal courts and tribunals and by the growing number of pronouncements of *national* courts on international crimes (such as war crimes, crimes against humanity, torture, genocide and terrorism), based on various heads of jurisdiction: territoriality, active nationality and universal jurisdiction.

The Reasons for the Increasing Importance of International Criminal Justice
....

WHY IS THE expansion of international criminal accountability a striking feature of the present world community? There are at least *three main reasons* for this healthy development.

Firstly, the demise of the cold war and the consequent end of the reciprocal diffidence entertained by the various blocs of states have made it possible not only to resort to dispute-settlement mechanisms previously untapped but also to impose the principle of individual accountability of state officials and other authors of international crimes and, by the same token, to set up international machinery designed to implement this principle.

Secondly, the growing weight of the human rights doctrine and the need to impose respect for such rights, coupled with the weakness of existing supervisory mechanisms, has proved that the most forceful way to react to appalling violations of human rights resided in going to the root of the problem: instead of taking on the State to which the offenders belonged, it was necessary to strike at the individual offenders themselves. Hence the gradual shift in emphasis from *State responsibility* to *individual criminal liability of state officials*. This was consistent with the famous Nuremberg dictum that 'crimes against international law are committed by men, not by abstract entities, and only by punishing individuals who commit such crimes can the provisions of international law be enforced'.[1]

Thirdly, there is a significant reason for the increasing resort to international criminal courts. On account of a number of political and military factors, the UN Security Council, the highest political body of the international community, is frequently unable to discharge two essential functions: (i) to provide specific parameters for the exercise by sovereign states of their *jus ad bellum* (namely their right to self-defence in case of armed attack, laid down in Article 51 of the UN Charter); (ii) to enforce compliance by states with the *jus contra bellum*, that is, with the UN Charter ban on resort to force in international relations (Article 2 para 4 of the UN Charter)[2]. As a consequence of this failure, the Security Council is increasingly turning to action that relates to *jus in bello*. Thus, being unable to stop resort to violence in international or internal relations or other serious threats to peace and security, the Security Council at least tries to impose *restraints* on such violence, by protecting civilians to the extent possible and providing for the prosecution and punishment of the authors of the gravest breaches of humanitarian law. This the Security Council does in particular by establishing ad hoc international criminal tribunals designed to stem the worst atrocities as much as possible (in this respect, suffice it to recall the ICTY and the ICTR).

The Current Outlook for International Criminal Justice

WHAT ARE THE realistic prospects for international criminal justice? Is it bound to gradually wane in the long period because of the widespread 'tribunal fatigue'? Or is it instead destined to flourish even more? If the second alternative is the more plausible, as I believe, what trends are likely to take shape in the next few years?

In light of current developments, I would suggest that in the near future, international criminal justice is likely to take *three different paths*.

A   The Increasing Effectiveness of the International Criminal Court

FIRST, THE ICC is likely to gradually move from its present stand, where it is still laboriously testing the waters and cautiously experimenting with its complex procedural rules, to a firm position where it will fulfil its important mission efficaciously. Particularly if the Prosecutor decides to stop waiting for the referral of situations by states or by the Security Council and begins to exercise the important and unique power he has been granted under the ICC Statute, namely to initiate investigations *proprio motu*, the Court's effectiveness is likely to increase. I should emphasise that initiating investigations *proprio motu* whenever a situation so requires does not necessarily mean that many more cases will be heard by the Court: the mere fact that investigations are launched and suspects or accused persons are named may 'shame' states enough to prompt them to initiate proper investigations and prosecutions themselves, thus adhering to and putting into effect the principle of complementarity, albeit in a more 'aggressive' form.

Should the Prosecutor take this approach, in the long run the Court's universal potential can be expected to bear fruits, by showing that it can be not only fair and impartial, but also expeditious in holding the major perpetrators of crimes accountable. This, I believe, would also result in a growing number of States gradually becoming parties to the Court's Statute. The ICC will thus come to occupy its rightful place in the constellation of international judicial bodies: it will constitute a judicial institution parallel to, and mirroring in its scope, the International Court of Justice. While one will continue to deal at the world level with interstate disputes, the other will handle – again at world level – issues relating to individuals' criminality.

B   The Expansion of National Courts' Prosecution of International Crimes

THE ICC RIGHTLY intends to be only *complementary* to the criminal jurisdiction of *national* courts, stepping in only when such courts prove unable or unwilling to repress international crimes. This is the second path that international justice is likely to take: the expansion of national prosecution and adjudication of war crimes, crimes against humanity, torture, genocide and terrorism. This expansion is justified, on two grounds. First, the courts of the State where a crime has been committed or of the State to which the alleged perpetrator belongs are those best suited to pass on the crime, for they are in a better position to collect the necessary evidence. Second, while international criminal tribunals for various reasons must concentrate on military and political leaders, namely those most responsible for crimes, national courts can also bring to justice the executioners and other 'secondary' perpetrators who indeed should be punished no less than those who masterminded, planned or instigated the crimes.

Unfortunately, however, on a number of political and practical grounds, courts in many states are loath to exercise territorial jurisdiction or to act upon the active nationality principle, even with respect to such atrocious, organized and large-scale offences as war crimes, crimes against humanity and other international crimes. As a consequence, the moral imperative –stemming from the human rights doctrine – not to let authors of heinous crimes go scot-free imposes resort to *extraterritorial* jurisdiction based on the universality principle. Indeed, exercise of such jurisdiction is bound to increase in importance.

I am fully aware that many states, particularly in Africa, claim that the universality principle is being used by Western countries, and especially by some European countries, as a subtle and pernicious way of interfering in the sovereignty of those African countries where the defendants live. African countries also insist on the emergence of a double standard in international criminal justice: in their view Western countries or other Great Powers whose state officials engage in war crimes or crimes against humanity in fact eschew any effective prosecution, because those countries have remained outside the ICC and in addition fail to prosecute their own nationals, without any judicial 'interference' of foreign states. In contrast, so the argument goes, nationals of African countries are brought to trial or at least accused either by the ICC or by the national courts of some European states. I feel that there is some truth in this double standard argument, although things are more complex and far from a black-or-white approach. A sound solution could be found in a two-pronged action. On the one hand, African states should be encouraged to exercise their jurisdiction effectively over their own nationals suspected or accused of international crimes. On the other, European states should be prompted to subject the exercise of their extraterritorial jurisdiction to a set of conditions designed to prevent international justice from causing undue interstate friction. To this effect, some recommendations recently made by a Working Group of 'Experts on the Principle of Universal Jurisdiction', appointed by the European Union and the African Union, should, in my view, be taken up by European countries.[3] For instance, when a European court has evidence that serious international crimes have been committed abroad by a foreign senior state official, before exercising universal jurisdiction it should (i) consider requesting the territorial or national State to prosecute the alleged offender, (ii) refrain in any case from taking steps that might publicly and unduly expose the suspect or accused, (iii) take into account the personal immunities that the suspect or accused may enjoy under international law; furthermore, (iv) where there is serious reason to believe that the territorial State or the State of the offender's nationality is unable or unwilling to prosecute him or to conduct a fair trial, the European court should try to issue a summons to appear rather that an arrest warrant, with a view to avoid exposing the foreign state official to public condemnation before trial.

C   The Establishment of Hybrid Criminal Courts

THE THIRD AVENUE that international justice is likely to take hinges on the establishment by the UN Security Council of ad hoc hybrid criminal tribunals entrusted with a *limited and very specific task* concerning some particular situations that *neither national courts nor the* ICC are able or prepared to tackle. There is a need for such hybrid courts when, for instance, existing international criminal courts and tribunals lack *temporal* or *subject-matter* jurisdiction over the crimes at issue and, in addition, although national courts per se are unable to dispense justice properly, the authorities of the relevant State wish their judges to have a say in the accountability process by participating in the adjudicatory proceedings. Various examples of such tribunals come to mind: the Special Court for Sierra Leone; the Special Panels for Serious Crimes established in East Timor; the Chamber for War Crimes created at the High Court in Sarajevo; the Internationalized Panels in Kosovo; the Cambodian Extraordinary Chambers; and the Special Tribunal for Lebanon.

These courts are intended to be *specially tailored* to the unique features of the crimes they are designed to handle. To be effective, such courts must also be different from most permanent judicial bodies, which are encumbered with a huge judicial apparatus; they should be lean and inexpensive as well as expeditious in their action. Given these characteristics, I believe that there is room in the future for the institution of these hybrid international courts, provided of course that those operating today prove satisfactorily to meet the special needs for which they have been established.

I am not unmindful of the objections frequently voiced against hybrid courts. The political decisions at their origin are often assailed: why set up a court with regard to a certain situation or country and not with regard to another, probably more serious, set of events? For instance, I am not unaware that in some Arab countries, many ask publicly why an international tribunal has been established to look into a string of terrorist attacks that occurred in 2004-2005 and possibly thereafter, while no tribunal has been created to deal with the 2006 short war in south Lebanon or the recent fighting in Gaza with all its exceedingly serious consequences in terms of attacks on civilian life and limb. As a judge, I can only answer that these are choices made by politicians. Once an international tribunal is set up, it is for its judges to act professionally and dispense justice freely and fairly, unfettered by any political consideration whatsoever. Let me add that similar considerations also hold true for national courts, although perhaps to a lesser degree: the initial decision to investigate and prosecute some classes of crimes is a political choice in many domestic systems, but then strictly and exclusively legal considerations become paramount once this choice is made and courts begin to discharge their institutional function.

Have the hybrid tribunals established so far lived up to the high expectations surrounding their creation? A general appraisal of so many and so diverse mixed judicial bodies is not easy. However, generally speaking those courts have proved helpful, although it is widely felt that some of them (in particular the Special Court for Sierra Leone and the Extraordinary Chambers in Cambodia) have not met – at least so far – the demand for swift and economic judicial action.

The Special Tribunal for Lebanon (STL), which has just been set up, must still be tested. Will it prove that it may initiate a new experiment in rapid, effective and inexpensive criminal justice? So far, the novelties of its Statute and its Rules of Procedure and Evidence have shown that significant innovations can be introduced in international justice with a view to making it more fair and efficient[4]. Let me draw attention in particular to five legal techniques adopted to streamline the procedure and render it very fair: (i) the new and original role assigned to the Pre-Trial Judge, who now not only manages pre-trial proceedings but also ensures that a wide range of legal issues are expeditiously and fairly settled so that trial proceedings can start promptly; (ii) the full implementation of the equality of arms principle realized by putting the Head of the Defence Office on the same footing as the Prosecutor; (iii) the broad role granted to victims that intend to take part in proceedings instead of testifying in court; (iv) a set of measures alternative to detention designed to give effect as much as possible to the principle that an accused is presumed innocent until conviction; and finally, (v) the modalities for accepting at the judicial level reliance on sensitive information affecting national security. This last point, in particular, should not be underestimated: indeed, when dealing with crimes of terrorism, investigations must rely on sensitive and confidential information, much more than in cases of war crimes or crimes against humanity, there therefore arises the need to put in place judicial mechanisms that ensure that the use of such information by one party to the proceedings does not jeopardize the rights of the other party.

These are clearly significant innovations that should enable the STL to remedy – at least to some extent – a number of flaws that have emerged in the practice of other international criminal tribunals. However, the STL must meet *two formidable challenges*. One is that the Tribunal is the first international judicial institution tasked to approach terrorism as a discrete crime. International terrorism is a protean notion, difficult to handle, also because there is no international case law on which to rely. The Tribunal should prove to be able to apply a sound and generally acceptable notion of terrorism in a well-balanced manner. The second big challenge is that the Tribunal is the first international criminal court operating within the Arab world. So far these countries have shown scant interest in, and in some instances have even cast a suspicious glance at, supranational criminal justice. To make them amenable to this system of justice would constitute a significant achievement. To do so, one ought to show beyond any reasonable doubt that international justice can be impartial, fair and immune from any political or ideological bias.

Only time will tell us whether this new attempt to bring justice into the international arena and open up new vistas will be successful.

Notes

....

*   This essay is based on a paper given on 8 June 2009 at The Hague Conference on International Justice organized by Professor C. Bassiouni. Although the author had been invited in his capacity as President of the Special Tribunal for Lebanon, the views set out here in no way reflect the position of any national or international institution.

1   *Trial of the Major War Criminals before the International Military Tribunal,* Nuremberg (Germany), 1947, vol. 1, at 223.

2   On this specific point see the apposite comments of L. Condorelli, *Some Thoughts on the Optimistic Pessimism of the Good International Lawyers* (forthcoming in the *European Journal of International Law*).

3   See the Report of the Working Group annexed to the document of the Council of the European Union 8672/09, REV.1, of 16 April 2009, §§ 46 and R1 through R17.

4   For a sketchy survey of the main novelties of the STL Rules of Procedure and Evidence, see the Explanatory Memorandum issued by the Tribunal's President, online: www.stl-tsl.org.

Is the Bell Tolling for Universality?*

A Plea for a Sensible Notion of Universal Jurisdiction

ANTONIO CASSESE

It would seem that the principle of universal jurisdiction over international crimes is on its last legs, if not already in its death throes.

The International Court of Justice (ICJ) delivered the first blow to universality in 2002 in its judgment in the Arrest Warrant case.[1] In addition to stating that foreign ministers enjoy personal immunity from jurisdiction while in office, the Court also held obiter that, after leaving office, such ministers may only be prosecuted for acts performed – while in office – 'in a private capacity' (à titre privé).[2] The range of criminal prosecution against foreign ministers (as well as, one can assume, any other senior state official) was thus significantly narrowed. As a consequence, the reach of national jurisdiction, including universal jurisdiction (the exercise of which by Belgian authorities had triggered the proceedings before the Court), was correspondingly reduced.

Subsequently, the only two instances of national legislation that uphold a very broad notion of universality, those of Belgium and Spain, have been considerably weakened. Following protests by the US authorities, the Belgian law of 1993/99 was amended in April 2003[3] and then again, more radically, in August of the same year.[4] In April the exercise of extraterritorial jurisdiction over crimes showing no link with Belgium was made conditional on a decision of the Belgian Federal Prosecutor; the law also envisaged the power of the Minister of Justice to hand over the case either to the International Criminal Court or to a competent foreign court. As a result of further complaints by the US Defence Secretary,[5] in August the law was amended again so as to completely expunge the principle of extraterritorial jurisdiction over international crimes and only uphold the active and passive nationality principle, plus the principle of legal residence in Belgium (for a minimum of three years).

In Spain on 25 February 2003, the High Court (*Tribunal Supremo*) in the *Guatemalan generals* case placed a restrictive interpretation on universality. It emphasized that universal jurisdiction may only be exercised as a subsidiary principle, namely if another relevant state (e.g. the territorial or national state) fails to act upon an offence, and provided that there is a link between the foreign offence and Spain. Such a link could be the Spanish nationality of the victims or the presence of the alleged offender in Spain.[6] Interestingly, following this judgment the investigating judge Baltazar Garzón, in his order of 29 June 2003 for the imprisonment of the Argentinian Miguel Angel Cavallo (extradited by Mexico to Spain), was keen to emphasize that both the fact that the victims of the crimes attributed to Cavallo included some Spaniards and the presence of the accused on the Spanish territory following his extradition from Mexico justified the exercise of universal jurisdiction by Spain.[7]

More recently, the Democratic Republic of Congo instituted proceedings against France before the ICJ. It claimed that the exercise of jurisdiction by French courts over some Congolese nationals, including the Head of State, for alleged torture, ran against international law.[8] Finally, on 4 April 2003 a US Court of Appeals excluded in *US* v. *Yousef and others* that the crime of terrorism could be subject to universal jurisdiction.[9]

Should we conclude that all these episodes signal the end of universality?

One fact cannot be denied: much confusion and uncertainty reigns over this intricate matter. Let us therefore see whether some clarification is possible by setting out a number of points on which some measure of agreement might be reached.

First, customary international law does not authorize states to assert criminal jurisdiction over offences perpetrated abroad by foreigners against foreigners (except perhaps when criminal conduct abroad may have serious consequences for a state, for example in the case of counterfeiting national currency). It stands to reason that if, say, a Pakistani engages in robbery in Karachi against other Pakistanis, a French court may not institute criminal proceedings against him, but only extradite him to Pakistan if the robber happens to be on French territory and France is asked for extradition. Both the concept of national sovereignty and common sense impede the exercise of French jurisdiction. The alleged robbery has caused harmful effects to the Pakistani community and amounts to a reprehensible breach of law and order in that State. Furthermore, the evidence is most likely to be found in Pakistan. On top of that, no French interest has been affected by the Pakistani robbery. Why then should a court sitting in Paris step in and bring the offender to trial? As far as 'ordinary criminal offences' are concerned, one could therefore be content with traditional criteria, chiefly territoriality and (active) nationality. The celebrated judgment of the Permanent Court of International Justice in *Lotus* dealt with this class of offences and ultimately relied upon territoriality.[10] It would seem that the above propositions hold true even though a trend is gradually emerging, at least in Europe, towards a weakening of the traditional principles of sovereignty and territoriality, to the benefit of trans-national integration (one may for instance think of the European arrest warrant, which, when issued in one European country, under certain conditions may automatically be executed in all the others).

Second, customary international law makes, however, an exception for some special classes of criminal offences that constitute attacks on the whole international community, that is, international crimes. These crimes infringe on values shared by all members of that community, as held in a string of cases from *Eichmann*[11] to *Guatemalan generals*[12] and *Ricardo Miguel Cavallo*.[13] It is therefore held justified that each state should be authorized to bring the alleged offender to book. General international law indisputably authorizes states to assert extraterritorial jurisdiction over piracy. It does the same with grave breaches of the 1949 Geneva Conventions. Although universal prosecution of those grave breaches is provided for in treaties, such treaties are by now binding upon all states of the world, except for two minor ones (Nauru and Marshall Islands), and on many grounds it seems very difficult for states to denounce the Conventions. What is more important, the icj has authoritatively held that the main provisions of those Conventions – which no doubt include the penal rules – have turned into customary international law.[14] It is therefore warranted to hold that, while the Conventions provide for both an *entitlement* and an *obligation* to prosecute (or extradite) alleged authors of those breaches, at least the *power* to prosecute those grave breaches is envisaged in general rules of international law. It has been argued that states are also allowed to assert universal jurisdiction over other crimes: genocide, crimes against humanity, war crimes (other than grave breaches of the Geneva Conventions) and torture. The judicial practice supporting this contention should not be neglected: see for instance *Yunis, Demjanjuk* as well as *Yousef and others*[15] or, with regard to torture, *Furundžija, Pinochet*, and *Simon Julio, Del Cerro Juan Antonio*.[16] Furthermore, the proposition is fully consonant with the general rationale behind the assertion of universal jurisdiction over international crimes.

Third, universality may be asserted subject to the condition that the alleged offender is on the territory of the prosecuting state.[17] It would seem contrary to the logic of current state relations to authorize any state of the world to institute criminal proceedings (commence investigations, collect evidence, and lay out charges) against any foreigner or foreign state official allegedly culpable of serious international crimes. In addition, some judges or authors have emphasized the serious disadvantages of this system.[18] This notion of universality postulated or advocated by, among others, the scholars behind the Princeton Project[19] and three distinguished judges of the ICJ,[20] may perhaps be reserved for the future, if and when international relations become more geared to the realization of universal values. At present, it could arguably be restricted to a few minor cases, not likely to spawn clashes between states.[21] Let me add a few remarks on the requirement that the alleged offender be present on the state's territory. In practice, this requirement implies that in most cases the suspect's (or accused's) presence may not be short (say for a brief holiday): otherwise, there would be no time to conduct preliminary criminal proceedings leading to the issuance of an indictment (however, the mere presence may suffice when criminal proceedings have already been instituted in another state, which requests the extradition of the alleged offender). It is notable that extraterritorial jurisdiction based on the presence of the suspect or accused is imposed by some international treaties (on torture and terrorism) under the *aut prosequi aut dedere* principle (a contracting state on whose territory the offender finds himself is bound to prosecute him, unless it decides to hand him over to another contracting state).

Fourth, it would seem that, at least at the level of customary international law, universal jurisdiction may only be exercised to *substitute for other countries* that would be in a better position to prosecute the offender, but for some reason do not (even after being consulted by the authorities of the *forum deprehensionis* about the reasons for not prosecuting the alleged offender). These countries are the territorial state or the state of active nationality: they may stake out a sort of 'primary claim' to jurisdiction, on account of their strong link with the offence or the offender). In other words, under customary international law, universal jurisdiction may only be triggered if those other states fail to act, or else have legal systems so inept or corrupt that they are unlikely to do justice. Universality only operates, then, as a *default* jurisdiction.[22] The logic behind this use of universality can be found in many treaties, including the four Geneva Conventions of 1949, the 1984 Convention against Torture, and many treaties on terrorism. Here, the contracting state is offered the choice between prosecuting the suspect or handing him over to a relevant country. An exception can be found in the four Geneva Conventions of 1949. There the primary obligation is that of prosecuting (hence the extraterritorial jurisdiction is not *substitutive* or *residual*, because the Conventions themselves enjoin the *forum deprehensionis* state to institute proceedings, thereby *reversing* the relationship existing under customary international law between the *forum deprehensionis* and the territorial or national state). True, as rightly pointed out by R. Higgins,[23] these treaties do not provide for universal jurisdiction proper, for only the contracting states are entitled to exercise extraterritorial jurisdiction over offenders present on their territory. In addition, it may be contended that such jurisdiction does not extend to offences committed by nationals of states *not parties*, unless the crime (1) is indisputably prohibited by customary international law (this holds true for torture, for instance, but not for terrorism, at least according to *Yousef and others*),[24] or (2) the national of a non-contracting state engages in prohibited conduct in the territory of a state party, or against nationals of that . Nevertheless, the fact remains that those treaties are important both on account of the high number of contracting parties and because they encapsulate the concept that states are entitled to sit in judgment over certain offences perpetrated abroad by foreigners.

Finally, customary international law contains a rule that protects alleged offenders who happen to be *incumbent* senior state officials. Heads of states or government, foreign ministers and diplomats, even if accused of international crimes, may not be prosecuted so long are they are in office (see in this respect, in addition to *Arrest warrant*, *Fidel Castro* as well as *Sharon and others*).[25] This shield of personal immunity is only removed when they leave office: at that stage they may then be tried for international crimes.[26]

Can the international rules referred to in the above propositions be regarded as sufficient to allay the worries of many states? More generally, do they strike the right balance between the interest of the international community in punishing those accused of horrific crimes and the will of states to safeguard their sovereign prerogatives and shelter their nationals from foreign interference?

Arguably, if the above safeguards are upheld, the exercise of universal jurisdiction by national courts is not likely to disrupt or jeopardize international relations, while it may instead powerfully contribute to the consolidation of international justice. Of course, if both the conditions on which the exercise of universal jurisdiction must be made contingent and the other limitations restraining this exercise were laid down in a *treaty*, much of the current uncertainties surrounding customary law would be dispelled. However, we cannot simply wait until such a treaty is hammered out. In the meantime, one is thus bound to rely upon a sensible construction of customary international rules.

In short, the cases and legislative amendments referred to above only sound the death knell for *absolute* universal jurisdiction (which one could also term "universality unbound" or "wild exercise of extraterritorial judicial authority"). Things are not bad for "conditional universality" – the moderate conception of universality as a default jurisdiction (or *justicia supletoria* – supplementary justice, as termed by the Spanish High Court).[27] Such jurisdiction may only be triggered when the territorial or national state fails to act, and provided the prosecuting state shows an acceptable link with the offence. This category of extraterritorial jurisdiction not only remains alive but is also susceptible to important developments, as suggested by Louise Arbour in her Editorial Comment in the Journal of International Criminal Justice of December 2003.

Admittedly, however much it may be restrained by the above safeguards, conditional universal jurisdiction, if upheld by an *increasing* number of states, is likely to lead to the prosecution of *former* leading politicians accused of very grave crimes (as well as *incumbent* senior officials not enjoying personal immunities). This would no doubt entail the subjection of (former or current) high-ranking dignitaries involved in actions showing a marked political dimension to the judiciary. The submission of high politics to judicial scrutiny may not be eschewed, however, lest one should leave unchecked misconduct involving large-scale murder, torture, persecution, or genocide. The *dilemma* is clear: either we take human rights seriously, which demands the consistent prosecution and punishment of those who grossly trample upon them, or else we only pay them lip service, in which case it is understandable that means of protecting state authorities from judicial investigation are devised.

Notes

....

*   This article has been published in the *Journal of International Criminal Justice* 1 (2003), 589-595.

1   International Court of Justice, judgment rendered on 14 February 2002 in *Case*

Concerning the Arrest Warrant of 11 April 2000 , at § 61. The text of the judgments is on line: www.icj-cij.un. org

2 See law of 23 April 2003, published in *Moniteur Belge*, 7 May 2003, at 24846-24853. Online at www.moniteur.be

3 See law of 5 August 2003, published in *Moniteur Belge*, 7 August 2003, at 40506-40515, Articles 13-16. Online at www.moniteur.be. It has been recently reported that the law has already been applied in at least one case: the Belgian Federal Prosecutor has rejected a lawsuit against China's former President, Jiang Zamin, by six Chinese plaintiffs, all members of the Falun Gong spiritual movement (*International Herald Tribune*, 9 October 2003, at 3).

4 See *International Herald Tribune (IHT)*, 23 June 2003, at 5; *IHT*, 24 June 2003, at 5.

5 See judgment (*sentencia*) of 25 February 2003, on line: www.derechos.org/nizkor/guatemala/doc/gtmsent.html, at 54 (in Spanish). See in particular Legal Grounds nos. 5-12, as well as the disposition (*fallo*), at 36. The High Court partially upheld an order (*auto*) by the *Audiencia Nacional* of 13 December 2000. It should be noted that under Spanish law, passive nationality is not a ground of jurisdiction.

6 See order (*auto*) of 29 June 2003 online: http://www.derechos.org/nizkor/arg/espana/cavallo3.html, at 3 (Legal Ground no.2). The Prosecutor had requested that Cavallo be released for lack of jurisdiction over his alleged crimes.

It is notable that in the order requesting the extradition of Cavallo, issued on 12 September 2000, the investigating judge had, however, simply relied upon the Spanish legislation on universal jurisdiction (Art. 23(4) of the Law on the Judicial Power): see the order online: http://www.derechos.org/nizkor/arg/espana/cavallo2.html), pp 128-138.3 (Legal Ground no. 2 of the section containing the "Legal Reasoning").

7 See ICJ, *Case Concerning Certain Criminal Proceedings in France (Republic of the Congo v. France)*, application of 9 December 2002, online: www.icj-cij.org.

8 *US v. Ramzi Ahmed Yousef and others*, US Court of Appeals for the Second Circuit, decision of 4 April 2003, in 327 F.3rd 56, at 78-884, also in 2003 U.S. App. LEXIS 6437, at 58-68. It should however be pointed out that the reason why the Court ruled out universal jurisdiction for terrorism was the 'indefinite nature' of this crime.

9 PCIJ, Judgment of 7 September 1927, Series A, no.10, at 19-31. The Court was called upon to pronounce upon a collision between the French mail steamer *Lotus* and the Turkish collier *Boz-Court* on the high seas off Mitylene, which caused the death of eight Turkish nationals. The Court held that Turkish courts were competent to adjudicate the matter for the collision had had effects on Turkish territory.

10 Supreme Court of Israel, decision of 29 May 1962, in 36 *ILR*, at 304.

11   Decision cited *supra* note 5, at 19 (Legal Ground no.5) and 25 (Legal Ground no. 8).

12   See the order of 29 June 2003 mentioned *supra* note 6. The investigating judge noted that genocide and terrorism "assault the very essence of humanity, and their victims are not only those directly affected but also the international community" (*atentan a la propia esencia del ser humano, y cuyas víctimas no solo son las inmediatamente afectadas, sino también la propia Comunidal Internacional*, at Legal Ground no.3).

13   See ICJ, Advisory Opinion of 8 July 1996 on *Legality of the Threat or Use of Nuclear Weapons*, §§78-82, in ICJ *Reports 1996*, at 257-8. See also the judgment of 27 June 1986 in *Case Concerning Military and Paramilitary Activities In and Against Nicaragua*, at § 220, in ICJ *Reports 1986*, at 114.

14   See *Yunis*, decision of the US District Court for the District of Columbia, decision of 23 February 1988, 681 F. Supp. 909(US); 1977 US Dist LEXIS 2262, at 903; *Demjanjuk v. Petrowsky and others*, US Court of Appeals for the Sixth Circuit, decision of 31 October 1985, in (1985) 776 F 2nd 571, also in 1985 US App. LEXIS 24 541; *US v. Ramzi Ahmed Yousef and others*, US Court of Appeals for the Second Circuit, decision of 4 April 2003, in 327 F 3rd 56, at 78-84, also in 2003 US App. LEXIS 6437, at 58-64.

15   See *Furundžija*, ICTY, Trial Chamber, decision of 10 December 1998, § 156; *Pinochet*, decision of the House of Lords of 24 March 1999 in [1999] 2 All ER, speeches of Lord Browne-Wilkinson (at 837-838) and Lord Millet (at 911-912); *Simon Julio, Del Cerro Juan Antonio*, Argentina, Federal Judge Gabriel R. Cavallo, judgment of 6 March 2001 (unpublished typescript on file with the author, 1-133, at 55-56).

16   While the presence of the accused on the territory of the prosecuting state is the crucial test for the exercise of universal jurisdiction, one might also accept another close link with the forum state, such as the legal residence of the alleged offender (this indeed seems to be the only acceptable link between the offence by one of the Congolese accused of torture before a French court and France, in the *Case Concerning Certain Criminal Proceedings in France (Republic of the Congo v. France)*, brought before the ICJ in 2002). Indeed, by choosing to have the legal residence in a foreign state, a person evinces the intention to be linked to that state and to submit to its laws.

The close link in question should not, of course, consist of the passive or active nationality, or the protective principle, for otherwise one would be taken back to the traditional principles of jurisdiction.

17   President Guillaume, in his Separate Opinion in *Arrest Warrant*, judiciously held that the system "would risk creating total judicial chaos" and in addition "would... encourage the arbitrary for the benefit of the powerful, purportedly acting as agent for an ill-defined 'international community'" (at § 15). For further critical

comments see A.Cassese, "Y a-t-il un conflit insurmontable entre souveraineté des Etats et justice pénale internationale?" in A.Cassese and M. Delmas-Marty (eds), *Crimes internationaux et juridictions internationales* (Paris: Presses Universitaires de France, 2002), 23.

18   See *The Princeton Principles on Universal Jurisdiction*, Princeton Project on Universal Jurisdiction (Princeton, N.J.: Princeton University Press, 2001), 67, at 27-30, 42-44, online: http://www.princeton.edu/~lapa/unive_jur.pdf.
It should be noted that under these principles, the presence of the accused is required for commencement of trial.

19   See the Joint Separate Opinion that Judges Higgins, Buergenthal and Koojimans appended to the judgment of the ICJ in *Arrest Warrant* of 14 February 2002, at §§ 59-61.

20   See the suggestions advanced *de lege ferenda* in my book *International Criminal Law* (Oxford: Oxford University Press: 2003), 291.

21   This point was emphasized by the investigating judge Garzón in his order of 29 June 2003 in *Miguel Angelo Cavallo*. He pointed out that Spanish courts were entitled to exercise jurisdiction because in Argentina Cavallo could not be prosecuted due to the Argentinian laws on amnesty (*supra* note 6, Legal Ground no. 3).

22   R. Higgins, *Problems and Process – International Law and How to Use It* (Oxford: Clarendon Press, 1994), 62-65. The comments by R. Higgins are cited approvingly in *Yousef and others*, decision cited *supra* note 14, at 44-45 (or 59-60).

23   Decision cited *supra* note 14, at 84-88 (or 64-68).

24   For *Arrest warrant*, see §§ 59-61: for *Fidel Castro* see the order (*auto*) of the Spanish *Audiencia nacional* of 4 March 1999, no. 1999/2723, Legal grounds nos 1-4 (Spanish text in CD Rom, EL DERECHO, 2003, Criminal case law. The Court held that it could not act against Fidel Castro because he enjoyed international immunities, adding that this ruling was not inconsistent with the Court's holding in *Pinochet*, for Pinochet was a former Head of State whereas Fidel Castro was a Head of State in office (see Legal Ground no. 5).
For *Sharon and others* see the decision of the Belgian *Cour de cassation* of 12 February 2003, online: http:// www.cass.be/cgi_juris/juris_cass_a1.pl, at 6-9. See there the concluding remarks of the General Prosecutor, Mr Jean de Jardin, of 23 January 2003, *ibid.*, at 1-6.

25   It would seem that a balanced approach to this matter may be found in the Joint Separate Opinion that Judges Higgins, Buergenthal and Koojimans appended to the judgment of the International Court of Justice in *Arrest Warrant*. They suggest (at § 59), with regard to the exercise of absolute universal jurisdiction, that (1) a state contemplating bringing criminal charges must first 'offer to the national state the opportunity itself to act upon the charges concerned'; furthermore (2)

the prosecutor or investigating judge must act in full independence, 'without any links to or control by the government' of the prosecuting state; in addition (3) there must be some sort of link with the state, a link that the three outstanding judges see in at least the persons related to the victims requesting the commencement of legal proceedings (while I submit that the presence of the accused on the territory at the time charges are brought and criminal investigations commence is also required).

26   Decision of 25 February 2003, *supra* note 5 at 33 (Legal Ground no. 10).

Index

Printed in Great Britain
by Amazon.co.uk, Ltd.,
Marston Gate.